The

The Great Evangelists

The Lives of George and Stephen Jeffreys

Desmond W. Cartwright

Marshall Pickering

Marshall Morgan and Scott
Marshall Pickering
3 Beggarwood Lane, Basingstoke, Hants RG23 7LP, UK

First published in 1986 by Marshall Morgan and Scott Publications Ltd
Part of the Marshall Pickering Holdings Group
A subsidiary of the Zondervan Corporation

British Library CIP Data

Cartwright, Desmond W.
Great evangelists: the remarkable lives of
George and Stephen Jeffreys.
1. Jeffreys, George 2. Jeffreys, Stephen
3. Revivals—Great Britain—History—20th
century 4. Pentecostal churches—Great Britain
—History—20th century
I. Title
269.24 BV3785.J3/

ISBN 0 551 01328 1

Text set in 10/11½pt Plantin by
Brian Robinson, North Marston, Bucks.
Printed in Great Britain by Hazell Watson & Viney, Aylesbury, Bucks

Dedication

For the past, to the memory of P. S. Brewster
For the present, to my wife Lillian
For the future, to our son Christopher

Contents

Introduction

The Llynfi Valley, some eight miles from Bridgend in South Wales,has seen many changes in recent years. The valley stretches from the peaceful tranquility of the ancient church at Llangynwyd dating from the thirteenth century to the bustling town centre, overlooked by slag heaps containing the remains of the industry of former times. At one time there were more than a dozen coal mines within the compass of the valley; now only one remains and its future is uncertain.

In the old cemetery at Llangynwyd, close by the church door, is the grave containing the mortal remains of Stephen Jeffreys, third son of Thomas and Kezia Jeffreys. Kezia was daughter of a Baptist minister whose brother Francis was a director of Llynfi Iron Works and Brown Street, off the present High Street, was named after him. Across the lane in the newer cemetery Kezia lies with her husband Thomas, daughter Margaret Ann and five sons, George, Oswald, Edward, Thomas and Haydn. Her younger son George lies some two hundred miles away in Streatham Cemetery, in South London.

The following pages tell the story of Kezia and Thomas's two sons, Stephen and George. Between the wars they filled the largest halls in Britain, sometimes for night after night. At times it was necessary for the police to control the crowds who waited hours for the doors to open in huge buildings so that they could see and hear these men.

The story begins in a South Wales Valley, less than a dozen years before the start of the present century. Another baby boy came into the world and he was named George after his brother, recently dead, who bore the same name.

When he was born his older brother Stephen, hardly past his twelth birthday, left school and joined his father in the local coal mine. It is to this family in relative obscurity that we look to trace the beginnings of a movement that was to have a dramatic effect upon the lives of thousands of people in the period between the wars. The effect of the brothers' ministry was to have repercussions as far afield as New Zealand, Australia, South Africa and on the continent of Europe, in Switzerland, Sweden and Holland.

This is the story of triumph out of tragedy. Many of the characters who helped to make this story are no longer with us. Others who were involved in the formative period are now advanced in years. Some of the details of this story may come as a surprise to some of our older readers.

My thanks are due to a number of people. First, to those Pentecostal pastors whose ministry not only led me to Christ but taught me what it meant to go and serve the Lord. To John Dyke, P.S.Brewster and J.T.Bradley. To many of those who knew the Jeffreys family from early times and who were willing to answer so many questions with patience and obvious enthusiasm. To Robert and Alice Tweed and W.Llewellyn Bell, as well as to the last survivor of the children of Kezia and Thomas Jeffreys, Mrs Chrisley Jenkins of Maesteg, a charming Christian lady.

Finally, to many of the students and researchers in the field of Pentecostal studies who first stimulated me to study the subject, when, as Editor of the *Elim Evangel*, I found myself being asked for information which proved difficult to supply, and which was far from clear when I started.

The story that is told here is based upon many letters to and from Stephen and George Jeffreys and many of their associates covering a period of more than forty years. Where material of a controversial nature has to be introduced, the relevant facts are culled from a mass of material, much of which has not been previously used. I have also researched in the British Library, the Newspaper Library, Colindale and in the County Record offices in Wales and England. In addition, my own collection of printed material is the largest collection on British Pentecostalism anywhere in the world. Extensive use has also been made of the archives of the Elim Pentecostal Church.

I wish to place on record my thanks to T.W.Walker, General Superintendant and the Executive Council for granting free access to this vast store of primary material. This story must be seen, however, as my own interpretation of these events and not as an 'official version'.

[illegible] Direction of P[illegible] [illegible] in the
world [illegible] made of the [illegible] of
the Fund [illegible]

[illegible] thanks to E. W. Wat[illegible]
[illegible] the [illegible] Committee [illegible]
[illegible] pattern
[illegible] interpretation
of [illegible]

1: The Dark Valley

According to *Kelly's Directory of South Wales (1906)*, Maesteg is some 198 miles from Cardiff and eight miles west of Bridgend. It is the main town of the Llynfi Valley, which is saucer-like at Maesteg's town centre 420 feet above sea level and overshadowed by a mountain that rises to a height of 1,823 feet. The roads continue to climb for a mile or two up to the district of Nantyffyon and on up to Caerau. From the top of the mountain it is possible to see (on a clear day) the Bristol Channel and even Caldy Island, near Tenby.

At the final quarter of the last century, when our story begins, the whole valley was in the throes of the second phase of the Industrial Revolution. Early in that century the higher slopes had been covered in trees, while the lower parts were dotted with small farms. The river was fed by many streams and springs. One of the old inhabitants of the valley, who died in 1933 at the age of eighy-nine, remembered that the women used to wash their vegetables in a river so clean it contained trout, eels and salmon that weighed up to twenty pounds. There had been some mining of coal as early as the sixteenth century but this was mainly confined to surface workings. A poem written in 1620 enthuses:

> 'And in Glamorgan's hilly partes
> Coal great lie doth abound;
> For goodness and for plenty too
> Its equal ne'er was found.'

The close proximity of iron ore and a plentiful supply of labour made it an ideal place for commercial exploitation.

In 1801, 800 people lived in the parish of Llangynwyd and almost half the population were engaged in farming. By 1871 the population had increased to almost 9,000. In 1901, Maesteg district had a population of 15,000 and this had increased to almost 25,000 by 1911. Many of the houses built by the iron works or colliery companies were small terraced dwellings of two bedrooms and two rooms downstairs. A stone staircase led to one bedroom through which one had to pass to reach the other. In the middle of the last century there was an average of twelve people to each house. One can imagine the unhealthy conditions that thousands had to endure. A native writer described the houses as 'box-shaped, plaster covered, often inconvenient and always ugly'.

In 1908 the death rate in Wales among the children of the poor was fifty-five percent as against less than eighteen percent amongst the rich. Kezia Jeffreys, before she died in 1929 at the ripe old age of seventy-eight, had buried two husbands and six of her twelve children. All her three surviving sons were ministers. Later in the same year that she died, the youngest of her sons would fill to overflowing the largest church in Wales.

To piece together the early history of the Jefffeys family is no easy task. They never sought publicity, they were one of the many large, respectable but poor families living in the upper part of the Llynffi Valley at the close of the last century. Thomas Jeffreys worked in the colliery for as long as his health would permit. He died in his home at 32 Picton Street on Tuesday, September 3rd, 1895 at the age of forty-seven. The cause of death was recorded as 'chronic bronchitis and cardiac failure'. Those were the days before due recognition was given to industrial diseases such as silicosis and pneumoconiosis. There was no compensation for his widow.

Stephen had joined his father at the pit not long after his twelfth birthday and he worked there, apart from during strikes and lock-outs, for the next twenty-three years. Miners worked long hours; in the winter the only time they saw the sun was after 2pm on Saturday and on Sunday. Sometimes strikes were protracted, one lasted for five months in 1898 and another went on for eight weeks in 1910. In 1912 there was great hardship during another extended strike. Several of the chapels, including Siloh, set up canteens to feed the miners and their hard pressed families. Pithead baths were unknown and parish relief offered little help. The necessary reforms in working conditions only came slowly. But a good worker could earn £2. 10s 0d in 1913. It was in Maesteg that minimum wages were first paid to miners working in difficult conditions. Much of the credit for this was due to Vernon Hartshorn, the local miners' agent who became their Member of Parliament in 1918 and became Postmaster General in 1924 and who, at the time of his death in 1931, was Lord Privy Seal in the second Labour Government.

There were chapels a plenty in the valley, many of which had been well attended. The Sabbath was treated with respect. Thomas Jeffreys and his family were members of Duffryn Chapel. This was built in 1868 after meetings were first held in the former Colliers' Arms. The first chapel on Duffryn Road, Caerau was used until a larger building was erected in 1897. There was a very close association between Duffryn Chapel and Siloh, Nantyffyllon and for some years they shared a minister. After the Jeffreys family moved again (the last surviving sister remembers that the family had lived in twenty-eight different houses) they attended Siloh, Nantyffyllon. George was in the Sunday School class and Stephen in the flute band. Glasnant Jones, who was minister of Siloh from 1901 to 1907 took a particular interest in the family. After he was married, Stephen lived opposite the chapel.

Of the 110 houses in Picton Street (where Stephen lived – it was later re-named High Street) at the turn of the century, ninety percent were Welsh speaking. By the time of the census of 1971 only seventeen percent of the population could speak the language. It was said at one time that eighty percent of the population of the valley were attached to some place of worship, though it should be noted that it was a probably very loose association in the case of many of the young people. The Revival of 1904-05 brought in a whole new generation of converts, two of these were Stephen and George Jeffreys.

2: The Revival and After

The story of the Welsh Revival is reasonably well known in Christian circles. What is not so well known is that the area most powerfully affected in the Revival was the district around Maesteg.

Evan Roberts and his helpers visited the Llynfi Valley on three occasions. On the first occasion there were 1,208 converts recorded. Only one other area recorded a higher figure. In the second visit in January 1905 another 2,115 were added. The third and final visit gathered in another 2,091. This brought the total to 5,414. Such a total was massive by any standard and the impact on the community was tremendous.

Even before the Revival there were a large number of chapels and churches in the valley. Many of these had to be enlarged as a result of the Revival. At the same time, there were a great many public houses throughout the length of the valley. A total of 107 have been traced. With the development of the local mining industry, particularly after 1899, public houses were frequently opened near to all the local collieries. In the view of Rev. John Evans, a famous Welsh Wesleyan minister in the last century, the district was,'worse than Sodom and Gomorrah'.

Following the Revival, Mr William Davies, Justice of the Peace and Chairman of the Maesteg Council reported:

> 'As regards sobriety, there is a remarkable improvement throughout the district. A brewer's traveller admitted to a friend of mine that the returns had fallen seventy-five percent. The 'tone' of the district has undergone great change, the street language being much improved. The

stillness of the early morning is broken by the hymn-singing of the colliers going to and returning from work, and late at night the air is full of the singing of the revivalists going home. There is practically no police work now, as quarrelling and drunkenness seem to be almost at an end. The chapels were never so well attended. I know dozens of men who had previously simply squandered their money, but who are now spending it on food and clothing for their families.'

Even *The Times* noted in its issue of March 7th 1905:

'During the six months before the Revival began the number of people summoned at Bridgend Police Court from Llynffi Valley numbered 700, but the average since the revival movement spread there, has been not more than two per week.'

In his historical account *The Welsh Revival of 1904,* Dr Eifion Evans records that the months of November and December 1904 were the best period of the revival. It was during this time that the deepest and most lasting work was done.

Stephen Jeffreys was working in the mine for fifteen years. On the day after Christmas in 1898 he had married Elizabeth Ann Lewis, daughter of Joseph Lewis of Navigation Terrace, Maesteg. Joseph Lewis was a collier and deacon of Siloh Independant (Congregational) Chapel. At this time Stephen's commitment to vital Christianity could best be described as nominal. It was the impact of the Revival and a real experience of conversion of some of his fellow miners that caused Stephen to consider his own position before God. He had been under conviction for several days, and after being present at a meeting in Siloh Chapel on Thursday, November 17th his feeling of unease increased. The matter was finally settled on the following Sunday morning, November 20th 1904. The preacher on that occasion was the minister of Siloh, Glasnant Jones.

Fifteen year old George made a commitment at the same time.

During the next few months the brothers involved themselves in the work of the chapel, though Stephen was less involved than his younger brother. He was a married man with the resposibility of bringing up his young family of two daughters and a son. When Kezia married again, George went to live with Stephen and the brothers remained particularly close from that time. Relations between the other members of the family was always friendly but not unduly intimate. They did not keep up any regular correspondence. When George became famous in later years all that the family would get was a telegram telling them that he would call. In the thirties when a rumour went around the London area that Stephen had died, George said that he had not heard the story and he asked his informant to let him know if this was confirmed. It was not so much that the brothers were estranged, but that the relationship was one of trust that enabled each to live their own self-contained life and keep their own circle of friends.

The minister of Siloh Chapel took a special interest in George Jeffreys. In later years he testified:

> 'At the open air revival services I always found young Jeffreys at my side. I was privileged to give him his early religious tuition and a splendid scholar he was. Superior to other lads, there was a character in his face: I knew he was a 'chosen vessel'. When I left Siloh, Maesteg in 1907 young Jeffreys was in business, and had he remained in that calling, I am convinced he would have become a merchant prince.'

In 1907, two years after the Revival, when Glasnant Jones removed to Cross Keys, there were many changes in the chapels. The number of converts in Wales up to January 1905 was according to the *Western Mail*, 70,000. A later estimate in 1909 said that the membership of Welsh nonconformity had increased by as much as 80,000. The sudden and rapid growth was not sustained however and within a short period of two years the membership had slipped back by some 20,000. In 1909 at the East Glamorgan Congregational Association meeting in Aberdare, the Presidential Address was entitled 'Religious Indifference'.

There were small groups within many of the chapels who sought to keep alive the enthusiasm of the Revival and they began to seek an outlet in informal gatherings. They became known as 'Children of the Revival'. Such groups existed in most of the denominations. Dr Eifion Evans says 'The faithful remnant within each denomination consisted mainly of the rank and file of revival converts'. The Jeffreys brothers joined one of these groups, they met in Duffryn Chapel, Duffryn Road.

While the Welsh Revival was drawing to a close, another movement was beginning 6,000 miles away in Los Angeles which would draw the attention of the wider world to the pentecostal experience. News of the Welsh Revival had been widely reported in the United States and a prominent minister from Los Angeles had visited Wales where he met Evan Roberts. His reports had stimulated interest in the city and letters to and from Roberts had led to an expectation that there might be a revival in that area also. There was at the same time an increasing interest in a deeper Christian experience that was known as the baptism of the Holy Spirit. To some, this involved a crisis of personal holiness but for others, it was linked with events described in the second chapter of the Acts of the Apostles where the physical experience is evidenced by speaking in tongues.

Under the ministry of a humble black preacher, William Joseph Seymour, a few people in a prayer meeting received the baptism of the Holy Spirit with speaking in tongues. Crowds gathered at the home, 214 North Bonnie Brae Street, Los Angeles. In April 1906, this group took over a livery stable-cum-lumber store that had previously been a

Methodist Church. It became known as the Azusa Street Mission. News of what was taking place in the Mission was carried around the world in a very short time.

On Wednesday, April 18th, 1906 a report of these events appeared in the *Los Angeles Daily Times.* The report appeared on the same day that the San Francisco earthquake took place. This caused a lot of interest and turned the minds of many people to the prophecy of Joel:

> 'I will pour out my spirit upon all flesh; and your sons and your daughters will prophesy. . . I will show wonders in the heavens and in the earth.'

Christian workers from many parts of America and from Europe visited the Azusa Street Mission where meetings went on almost non-stop for two years. Their magazine, *Apostolic Faith,* which first appeared in September 1906, carried the news to all parts of the world. One of those who read this first issue was an English-born Norwegian Methodist minister who was in New York at the time. As a result of reading this first issue of the paper, and subsequent correspondence with the leaders of the Mission, T.B. Barratt also received the baptism of the Holy Spirit in a meeting in New York. His description is dramatic:

> 'There were not many people in the evening meeting, but God's power was mightily manifested. I asked the leader of the meeting. . . to lay hands on me and pray for me. Immediately the power of God began to work in my body, as well as in my spirit. . . my being was filled with light and an indescribable power, and I began to speak in a foreign language as loudly as I could. . . I am sure I spoke seven or eight languages. They were clear and plain. . . .The most beautiful of all was the singing – when the inspiration reached its climax, I burst out in a wonderful baritone solo, I never heard the tune before, and did not understand the words, but it was the most beautiful language, so smooth and easy to

pronounce. . . I shall never forget how beautiful and pure the singing sounded.'

Barratt was a talented musician and a student of Edvard Grieg, and the fact that this experience had such a powerful effect upon him tells us a great deal about the nature of his experience.

Within a short time Barratt returned home to Norway and his ministry made a dramatic impact, not only upon his own city mission but upon Christian work in the whole country, and indirectly also upon Sweden, Denmark and Britain.

The Pentecostal Movement in Britain began as a result of the interest of an English Anglican minister from Sunderland, Alexander A. Boddy. Boddy had visited Wales at the time of the Revival and he had stood alongside Evan Roberts in his meetings in Tonypandy, in the Rhondda Valley. He had returned to his church at All Saints, Monkwearmouth, Sunderland with a longing that such a revival would take place there. When he read of the reports of what was taking place in Norway in some of the English papers early in 1907, he determined to go and see for himself. What he saw made a deep impression on him. Boddy felt sure that Barratt's ministry was just what was needed in Britain and in his own parish in particular. He urged Barratt to come to Sunderland. Barratt came by ship and with a strong wind behind it the boat arrived early and he was in time for the meeting on Saturday, August 31st, 1907. He stayed for seven weeks and lived at the vicarage.

The meetings were rather quiet for the first few weeks. In that period a total of less than twenty had the experience known as the baptism of the Spirit. Amongst their number were the vicar's wife, Mary and his two daughters, Mary and Jane. Boddy himself had to wait until December 2nd, after Barratt had returned to Norway. The first month was very quiet. One night at the end of September, a reporter from the *Sunderland Echo* came to see what was taking place in the Parish Hall. His report on September 30th was picked up by one of the London papers and within a few days the vicarage was besieged by hungry newsmen. Vicar Boddy found himself the object of considerable curiosity.

There is not space here to tell of all the repercussions of these events, but one of the things which came from these meetings was an Annual Convention, meeting for the first time in the following Spring. It was from these events that the British Pentecostal Movement began to develop.

Things were also beginning to stir in the Welsh valleys. In Monmouthshire, close to Ebbw Vale, a Congregational minister, Thomas M. Jeffreys (no relation to the brothers) warmly welcomed preachers with Pentecostal leanings and several young men were baptised in the Spirit. A group from Dowlais, Merthyr and Aberaman in the Aberdare valley visited his church at Waunllwyd. Further west, Dan P. Williams, another convert of the Revival was led to hold special meetings in Penygroes, where he would eventually establish the Apostolic church which was to open many assemblies in Wales.

In the Llynffi Valley in 1910 there was a thirty-six year old Welsh Baptist minister named William George Hill of Calfaria, Cwmfelin, Maesteg. He was minister there from 1909-1910. Before he became a minister he had been a talented choirmaster and had won several competitions, including one with a a prize of £50. He ran into problems because he was against his church holding concerts in order to raise funds. He objected to a cantata being held in Maesteg Town Hall. When the event was held it only made a profit of six old pence after the deduction of expenses.

Mr Hill was also very sympathetic towards Pentecostal teaching and his own teaching ministry gave considerable encouragement to some of the early Pentecostal groups. He eventually resigned from the chapel and from the denomination and held meetings in the home of Mr and Mrs Bedford in Bridgend Road, next door to the Cross Inn. They also held meetings in Oakwood School, close to the chapel. George and Stephen Jeffreys attended these meetings.

3: Your Sons and Daughters

Stephen's son Edward went on holiday to Crosshands, near Ammanford and during his time there he, '. . . received a definite baptism of the Holy Spirit and began to speak in other tongues as the spirit gave . . . utterance'. He returned home to Maesteg and a few days later, a man who had been present at the meeting in Crosshands visited his parents and told them what had taken place. When the Pentecostal manifestations first appeared in the vicinity, George had spoken against them. Stephen and his wife Elizabeth had not been in favour of such things either. However, when they saw the beneficial effect that this experience had upon their younger son they began to view things in a more favourable light.

Not long afterwards, George was in the old Duffryn Chapel before the start of the Sunday morning meeting. According to his testimony, recorded in 1918 by a godly Church of Ireland minister, Thomas Hacket of Bray, the brothers confessed their wrong. On the same morning George began to sing in tongues and to magnify the Lord. From the time that he was a child, George had felt that he would be a minister. When he was a very small boy he used to play at conducting services. His father took him to see the well-known Swansea phrenologist, Professor Williams whose diagnosis was usually favourable. In George's case he gave promise of a bright future (he probably did the same for most parents, which would account for his popularity). George's father did not live to see many of his sons grow up. The only ones to live to be much more than thirty years of age were the three who became preachers; Stephen,

George and William. (Stephen's son Edward and William's son , Emlyn George also became ministers).

Both as young lads and as they grew up, Stephen was always the strongest. When he worked on the rich Victoria seam, deep in the bowels of the earth, Stephen threw all his energy into the backbreaking toil.

George looked frail; as he grew up Kezia was determined that he would not go down the coal mine. He went to work at the Co-op stores in Nantyffyllon where he began as an errand boy. He was a good worker and a few years later the possibility of important promotion was to be a temptation when the call to the ministry became strong.

There were several obstacles to be overcome before Kezia's favourite son could be a man of the cloth. The first, and most serious obstacle was his health. His weak state manifested itself in a facial paralysis which pulled the muscles to one side, and in addition he had a speech impediment. Being somewhat reticent George suffered in silence. When he was in prayer at nine o'clock one Sunday morning, he received such an inflow of divine life that the only way he could describe it was as if his whole body had been connected to a powerful battery. He was completely healed and the old trouble never came back. In later years, when he proclaimed Jesus Christ to be the healer of the body and the baptiser in the Holy Spirit, it was much more than a theory to him. He now had an argument that was backed up by experience. It was natural that, following these two events, he should become increasingly drawn to Pentecostalism.

In August 1910 George wrote to William Oliver Hutchinson, a former army sergeant who had a Pentecostal Church in Bournemouth which was opened in November 1908 (it was the first Church to be built and opened as a Pentecostal Church in Britain). This contact was made through James Brooke, a former Baptist minister from Bournemouth who had joined Hutchinson's group and was in charge of the work at Belle View Chapel, Swansea. The letter is particularly interesting:

'Dear Pastor Hutchinson,
I really think that God would have me bear my testimony to the glorious work He has done in me, Hallelujah. Since I have been at Bournemouth. 'all things are become new–old things have passed away'. Hallelujah. I have been saved, sanctified, baptised in the Holy Ghost with the Scriptural sign of the tongues, Mark xvi.17 and healed of sickness. This is the Lord's doing, and it is marvellous in our eyes. Glory to God: God has taken the cigarette from between my lips, and put a Hallelujah there instead. Hallelujah.
I have the gift of tongues and interpretation; but the latter gift must still be developed.
I cannot tell you all he has done for me, as no tongue can glorify God sufficiently. I feel free and happy; so very joyful and anxious to do something. Now comes my testing. I am going home to Wales, and it is but the beginning of a mighty battle. But 'Lion of the Tribe of Judah' does not tell me to fight alone but he himself will do the worst part, and victory is always His. I thank you for your prayers. G.J.'

Hutchinson published the letter. The initials thinly disguised its author, who was then virtually unknown.
A few months later we meet the brothers again. They wrote to Price Davies, another convert of the Revival who was converted on the same day as Stephen. He was one of the band of young men who were brought under the influence of T.M. Jeffreys and who had come into a pentecostal experience. In their letter the brothers asked Price Davies if he would journey over from Dowlais to baptise them by immersion. Price Davies tells us that:

'Sunday morning three weeks before Easter 1911 (March 26th) Stephen Jeffreys . . . and Eddie Jeffreys his son were baptised in water under an open heaven . . . George Jeffreys was not baptised that morning . . . That week I had a letter from George saying that he was very sorry

> that he had not been baptised at the same time as Stephen and Eddie and asking if I would please come over and baptise him . . . George was not in the Sunday morning service but he was there for the evening and we closed that meeting early and marched in procession down through Bridgend to the river. There again under the open heaven George Jeffreys was baptised with a nice congregation joining in the service.'

The date was Sunday, April 11th, 1911. Any thoughts that George might have entertained about entering one of the denominational colleges to train for the ministry could now be put out of his mind.

The valley had been the birthplace of more than 150 ministers (of these, fifty-eight were Congregationalists and forty-eight Baptists). Bridley Richards (who was a solicitor and Stephen Jeffreys' executor) in his, *History of the Llynffi Valley,* (1982), states 'It is doubtful whether any valley of comparable size and population in Wales has made a greater contribution towards the maintenance of the Christian religion and the propagation of the Gospel'. The Jeffreys family would eventually muster seven ministers when brothers, sons and nephews are counted; all of them belonging to the Pentecostal Church.

Help was at hand in the person of Cecil Polhill, the wealthy squire of Howbury Hall, Bedford. Polhill had been a member of the 'Cambridge Seven', a group of notable Cambridge graduates, who had captured the imagination of the Christian public when they had sailed together to China on a missionary service in 1885. In 1903 Polhill had inherited a fortune and several thousand acres of land. After some years of missionary service in China and Tibet, he was invalided home. In the following years he made several prolonged visits to China. During a return visit in the early part of 1908, he went to Los Angeles and he visited the 'Upper Room Mission' of George B. Studd, brother of C.T. Studd. It was in G.B. Studd's home on February 3rd, 1908 that Cecil Polhill came into a pentecostal experience.

On his return to England, he made contact with many of the Pentecostal leaders and he helped to finance many of their early efforts. He became President of the Pentecostal Missionary Union, founded in Sunderland in January 1909. They opened several training homes for prospective missionaries and after a time, a finishing school for men students in Preston. The school was led by estate agent Thomas Myerscough, leader of a devout company of bible students who had been associated with the Brethren for many years. He had been brought into contact with pentecostal teaching through Henry Mogridge of nearby Lytham. After hearing of their work in Lytham, he went to see what was happening and he was deeply impressed. As a follow-up to this he went to the Sunderland Convention where he was baptised in the Holy Spirit at Whitsun, 1909. Myerscough was a man of wide experience and sound judgement and he was a natural 'father' to many of the young men who attended his Bible School.

In September 1912, the Council of the Pentecostal Missionary Union gave consideration to an application from George Jeffreys and recommended that he should go to Mr Myerscough's school in Preston. According to their records he began there in November 1912. A few days before he was, '. . . set apart for the regular work of the ministry' at a meeting in Maesteg on Thursday, November 13th. Several of his fellow students were to figure in his life in later years. By any standards they were a remarkable group of young men.

William F.P. Burton, son of a sea captain and three years George's senior was to pastor the Elim Mission at Lytham, prior to going to the Belgium Congo as a missionary. Robert Ernest Darragh from Bangor, Co. Down in Ireland, also three years his senior would be his closet companion for almost forty years. Ernest John Phillips from Bedford, whose father helped to run the Costain Street Mission there, would prove invaluable when their new group began to acquire property because of his early training in an estate office. From England, Ireland, Scotland and Wales, young men came to sit at the feet of Thomas Myerscough. From that small school they went out to conduct meetings both near and far. It was a good training ground for the small group of men and it is doubtful whether any school has ever had a group of students who have achieved so much in view of the short time that they were in Bible School. They had a very high success rate, higher by far than any of the other Pentecostal Bible Schools in the early period.

As things turned out however, George was to be there for a very short time and, once again, the reason had something to do with his brother Stephen.

4: The Making of Missioners

A short time before he went to Preston, George had been ministering to a small group in the Swansea Valley. The small company had enjoyed his ministry and wanted to book him for further meetings in October. He was reluctant to commit himself because of the uncertainty over the prospect of his going to Bible School. He recommended that they should invite his brother Stephen. Stephen had not done much preaching and at that time his strength lay in his ability as an open air preacher rather than in taking a complete church service. Some of the group asked Stephen to preach for them when they met him on a Saturday night at a service in Swansea. He accepted and preached for them on the following day and they found his ministry refreshing. As a follow-up they asked him to be their preacher at special meeting over the Christmas holidays of 1912.

The Mission had started in 1905 with a small Sunday school work amongst a needy group of neglected families in Cwmtwrch, some fifteen miles from Swansea. As a result, the leaders of the Sunday school were asked to leave their former place of worship and so they built a tin chapel at great sacrificial cost. Opened early in 1912, it was called Tro'r Glien Mission. There were only about fifteen members and they had no minister at first. They were glad for any able and faithful preacher to fill their pulpit. Thus, George Jeffreys used, at times, to occupy their pulpit. Stephen was still working in the coal mine. However, he had seen a few converted as a result of his ministry, including one of his fellow miners. The invitation to preach at the mission presented a new challenge but he took it in his stride. At 8 a .m . on a Sunday morning he went out into the quiet streets of the village where, in a loud voice, he called out a few verses of Scripture. It made a great impact and the congregation that day was considerably increased as a result of his bold summons to worship.

Stephen's second visit was arranged for Christmas Day, 1912 and it was intended that the meetings should continue over the weekend. Such was the blessing of God upon the meetings that Stephen was urged to continue. Converts were registered in almost every meeting and he had to get in touch with his friends in Maesteg to assist with the singing and testimonies. Stephen did the preaching. Three days went into a week and then on into the next week, with no sign of an end Stephen became desperate, he had never preached so many times without a break. Something had to be done, a solution had to be found and so an urgent despatch was sent to his younger brother George at the Preston Bible School. He came right away and entered into the work with a will.

The meeting went on for seven weeks. The Christian press carried the story of the mission, and early in February *Life of Faith*, the chief periodical of the Keswick Movement, carried a report headed, 'Wales in the Dawn of Revival'. One of the many who went to see what was taking place was Cecil Polhill who reported the meeting in his paper, *Flames of Fire.* At the time of writing his report there were 130 converts, thirty of whom had spoken in tongues. There were also a number of cases of miraculous healing. On the final night, the total number of converts reached 145. Alexander Boddy of Sunderland wrote asking about the meetings and the reply from George was published in his paper, *Confidence.*

Urgent invitations came for the brothers to conduct meetings in other places. In response to one such invitation from a Quaker magistrate in Radnorshire, some fifty miles away, they moved their sphere of operation. The new district was so different: Penybont, some five or six miles from Llandrindod Wells, was an upland agricultural district that was thinly populated. The meeting place was a three hundred year old thatched Quaker meetinghouse.

The meetings began on Monday February 17th, 1913. When the brothers first arrived they were unable to take in the remoteness of the location, they must have felt much the same as the evangelist Philip when he stood on the road to Gaza (Acts 8). They need not have worried, for in spite of the remoteness of the location the crowds began to arrive from every direction by car, bicycle and on foot. As numbers grew several different chapels were used; both brothers speaking and young Edward singing. An English visitor gives the following description in a letter that was written at the time:

> 'From the first time I saw them I was much impressed with their earnest manner, and felt that they were men with a special message given them by God to deliver. The meetings are conducted very simply and quite open, but in a reverent spirit. They don't press people to respond to the invitation to pray or give a testimony. They only say that if any will take part they shall be blessed in doing so and in confessing Christ. And, again, at the end of the meeting there is no urging of people to go to the front or to the enquiry room. Mr George Jeffreys is a fluent speaker, with a good delivery. He speaks as a well-educated man, and is intensely in earnest. He generally speaks first. After a chorus and prayer, his brother Stephen gets up: an entirely different style, but what a wonderful power! There is great power with George, but I feel it more intense in Stephen. I cannot explain it. One wonders how the people can sit still under such plain preaching. There were six conversions – definite cases that came out on Tuesday night. On Wednesday they paid a private visit to Llandrindod Wells. The people heard of it, and immediately bills were printed and distributed, and the brothers were urged to address a hurriedly assembled congregation, when four local ministers also took part,

and there was a blessed time. The meeting at Penybont the same evening was a very powerful one.'

Two weeks later, another writer interviewed the brothers and expressed himself as:

'. . . favourably impressed with their natural frankness, joyousness, and eagerness to be used in the salvation of souls, Stephen Jeffreys . . . is a simple, humble, and yet intelligent, level-headed man of a superior South Wales miner type. He is more at home conversing in Welsh than in English, though he has a fair command of the latter language. He protested that he was not a preacher, but simply delivered what he was taught in the Word of God and prompted by the Spirit to declare, together with his personal testimony the great work of grace wrought in his own soul in the Revival of 1905 and ever since.'

There were about fifty-one converts in this mission. There was also an outstanding miracle of healing.

Edith M. Carr of Caxton House, Llandrindod Wells, whose father was a draper, had been lame with a diseased foot for about nine months. She walked with a crutch and spent most of her time lying on a couch. Her surgeon feared that it would be necessary to amputate her foot. She was a believer and she asked her mother if the evangelists would come and pray for her. They went to her home and she was anointed with oil in accordance with James 5:14-15:

'Is any sick among you? let him call for the elders of the church: let them pray over him anointing him with oil in the name of the Lord; and the prayer of faith shall save the sick, and the Lord shall raise him up.'

The brothers had prayed for the sick in Cwmtwrch and a few people had been healed, but nothing of a dramatic nature had taken place: on this occasion it was to be different. Alexander Boddy, having published a report of the Cwmtwrch meetings in his paper, he decided to travel from Sunderland to Radnorshire to see things for himself. He went to the meeting unannounced and he was very favourably impressed by what he saw. He met Mrs Carr and her daughters and he quotes Edith's letter:

> 'A great light came round me, and filled me with great power, and I arose from the couch and stood on both feet, and walked gently round the room with scarcely any help.'

That evening Edith gave her testimony in the meeting and, according to Edward Jeffreys, Stephen's son, she offered her services as pianist and played the piano for the remainder of the campaign. The news of her healing created considerable interest and people came from far and wide to see what was taking place.

For the brothers, this was the first outstanding miracle of their ministry. It was to be the first of a string of remarkable cases which would form an important part of almost every subsequent mission they conducted during the next twenty years. The record of these cases is outstanding and in a great many cases they helped to effect a breakthrough when the meetings were hard going. The healings in themselves did not bring salvation either to the recipients, or to the crowds who flocked to see these things repeated or to gaze in wonder at the walking miracles.

Donald Gee, who later became the Secretary of the World Pentecostal Conference, but who, in 1921, was pianist for one of Stephen Jeffreys' campaigns wrote:

> 'Our faith in Divine healing accompanying evangelism on the line of *sign gifts* as a gracious possibility for our own day, and until the end of the age, has been remarkably vindicated by bold and faithful preachers whose huge meetings have provided the impressive answer to those who wonder how men and women can still be attracted to hear the Gospel. Healings do not

necessarily convert; they do not necessarily produce repentance unto life; they never take the function pertaining to the Word, and the Word alone; but they DO attract men to at least hear the life-giving word.' (*Trophimus I Left Sick (1952), p.9.)*

Once again, demands for the brothers services began to come in from all quarters. Many of Stephen's efforts would be concentrated in Wales where he felt more at home. George went to London where he stayed at the home of Mrs Margaret Cantel at Highbury New Park. She was the daughter of Mr Fielding, one of Dr Dowie's elders from Zion City, Illinois. Her husband, Harry Eugene Cantel, had been leader of a Pentecostal Assembly in Islington where he exercised a very successful ministry, until his sudden death in August, 1910 at the age of forty-four. Mrs Cantel took over a large house that was used as a meeting place and guesthouse for Pentecostal people who came to London from all over the world. It was in this same house that Donald Gee was to receive his pentecostal experience in March 1913. George stayed at 'Maranatha' from March 24th to May 16th. Stephen's son Edward stayed there with his uncle until May 8th and he sang in some of the meetings. Services were held in a variety of halls; the Welsh Wesleyan Church, City Road; Arundel Square Congregational Church (where D.L. Moody the American Evangelist had held his first London meetings) and finally in Holborn Hall for ten days. There were good meetings but George did not take London by storm. The conquest of sections of the great metropolis was more than a dozen years away. There was a long road ahead, much hard work, and not a few disappointments as well as much privation before the London papers would report, 'London Audience Mesmerised' on its billboards in 1927.

5: Some Pastors, Some Evangelists

In response to their preaching, the brothers were invited by Alexander Boddy to take part in the Sunderland Convention of 1913. George went along with a group from Wales, who made a considerable impact and created a powerful impression upon many of the visitors to the Convention. A report of George's preaching in a German Pentecostal paper drew attention to the important part that their preaching and singing played in open-air ministry.

> 'The twelve Revivalists from Wales took a great part in making this Convention full of life . . . To get a right idea of them it is necessary to hear them sing, then one can imagine how the revival was called a "Singing Revival". These brothers are a "peculiar people". They do not seem to have much inclination to give great speaches on teaching lines, but they are in their element when they are in the street and in public places starting a fiery Revival meeting; there they speak and testify again and again. On Whit Monday, May 12th, George spoke in the main hall which was crowded to the doors with an overflow into the streets. On Wednesday he gave a Gospel address on Isaiah 38:8 "The turning back of the shadows".'

He also preached at a Methodist Church and to the Salvation Army. It was in a Methodist Chapel in nearby Silkworth that a young boy gave his heart to Christ. He recalled the event nearly seventy years later when writing from rural Norfolk in a testimonial for a young man who had applied for the ministry of the Elim Church.

George also visited Leeds where he held meetings for the Mount Tabor mission. This was a small group who had been meeting in difficult circumstances in a needy area of the city since 1904. The difficulties were increased by a strike in the city and the meetings had to be conducted by candle and lamp-light. In spite of the problems the church was reorganised as a result of the success of these meetings and from that time they never looked back. A feature of the meetings was the many remarkable healings which took place. Seven years later George would pay another visit to the city when he saw even greater success.

Stephen was invited to hold a series of meetings in the Baptist Church at Llanelly. The minister, Trevor Jones was favourably impressed and Stephen found a favourable response to his preaching in the town and he decided to stay. He took over the pastorate of Island Place Mission. He remained there for the next seven years and was very happy. Often, during that time he would be seen going to and from the town station with his travelling bag. Time and again he would go away in response to a call from some small, struggling Mission. He would return home tired but happy with fresh stories to tell of souls saved and sick people healed.

On the first Sunday in July, 1914 (July 5th), there occurred one of the most remarkable incidents in his ministry. Stephen was preaching on the text in Philippians 3:10, 'That I may know him, and the power of his resurrection, and the fellowship of his suffering', he was aware of a special anointing upon his ministry and when he had concluded his message his wife beckoned him to come to where she was sitting. On the wall just behind where he had been preaching and a little to his right, there appeared a remarkable picture. At first, while he continued preaching, there was no clear outline, but as he went on a clear outline in the form of a face of a lamb began to appear upon the wall. This was clearly seen by many of the congregation and it was this that Elizabeth wanted Stephen to see. After he had finished his message several of the people went up to examine the wall. One man suggested that it was caused by the reflection of the electric light but he was answered, for when the pastor had the lights extinguished the picture was still clearly visible. After a time it changed to the appearance of Christ as the Man of Sorrows. The vision remained on the wall for some six hours, all told, where it was seen by hundreds of people. The caretaker eventually locked up the building at about two a .m ., though he still slipped back to have another look and found that it was still there. On the following morning, when Stephen went back there was nothing to be seen.

During the week one of the local papers sent along a reporter who talked to many of the people who had been present at the time. Reports appeared in a number of local papers, including the *Daily Citizen*, the *Llanelly Argus* and the *Llanelly Mercury* as well as the *Star* and the *County Guardian*. A photgraph was taken shortly afterwards and this was published. It did not reveal anything of an unusual nature as it was taken after the event. It is interesting, however, as it shows Stephen in the pulpit and an X marks the spot where the vision appeared.

On the last Sunday in July Stephen preached a powerful message on the text, 'This is the beginning of sorrows' (Matthew 24:8). Before that week was out the First World War commenced. What did it mean? For the whole of Europe the next five years were to be years of sorrow, pain and suffering. Llanelly, together with many other towns and villages in Britain had their share of suffering as fathers and sons went to fight on foreign fields: many never returned. Some of the boys were known to Stephen and not a few of them were his converts.

Jimmie Allen was a dropout living in a makeshift tent on a rubbish tip, scratching a living amongst the garbage. He was dirty, half-starved, more animal than human. Turned out of home because they could not cope with him, he was drunk whenever he could get hold of enough money to buy drink. One Sunday morning Jimmy found his way to Island Place and spoke to the man at the door. 'Can I come in?', he enquired. 'Is there a welcome for me here? I'm so tired of it all.'

'Of course there's a welcome for you Jimmie', the man said, 'Come along in.' At the end of the meeting Jimmy found his way to the front where he knelt down with his arms outstretched seeking forgiveness. Then he went to his own home and on the following Sunday he was back at the Mission but this time he was a new person. He was washed, shaved and clothed in a good suit and a smart collar and tie. Not only was there a change in his dress but deep down inside he was a new man. When general conscription was introduced Jimmie was called up along with many others in the town. He was sent to France where he fell on the battlefield.

George's preaching in Sunderland made a very favourable impression upon one of the Gillespie brothers from Belfast. William Gillespie had been converted in 1907 through the preaching of an American Pentecostal evangelist William Anderson. William Gillespie had gone to the Sunderland convention in 1913 where he had heard George Jeffreys preach. When he got back home to Pine Street, Belfast, he spoke to his brother George and they wrote inviting George Jeffreys to Ireland to hold meetings. They enclosed three ten shilling notes for his boat fare. The decision to go to Ireland was to be a momentous one. Not that everything went well at first. When they first sought to hold meetings in Monaghan they were rebuffed. The Methodist Hall that they had booked was refused them when it was discovered that they were Pentecostals. The first mission there had to be abhorted even though the leaflets had been printed.

After holding a few meetings and preaching at a convention in Belfast, George resumed his itinerant ministry. Times were hard and he travelled many miles during the year. In July and August he held meetings in Bangor, Co. Down. One of the Preston students, Robert

Ernest Darragh from Bangor returned there in February 1915 to work in the home of Mr Alex Ferguson. He was to be the first to join George when he returned to Ireland in 1915.

One of the first places where George preached was at Emmanuel Baptist Church, Plymouth for the minister, Edwin W. Bacon. There were a number of outstanding miracles of healing at these meetings. At the end of 1914 he held a fourteen-day mission at the Smithson Mission. Coulsdon. This was a branch work attached to the Holiness Mission of Pastor Inchcomb in Croydon. An outstanding feature of this mission was the conversion of George Miles, a railway ganger who worked on the London to Brighton line. His son, who became the distinguished minister of Bridge Street Church,Leeds, told the story of his father's conversion some sixty years later.

Mrs Miles was a devout Christian and was praying for her husband's conversion. She tried to get him to come to the meetings but he refused to do so. Whenever the Mission was mentioned the atmosphere became tense. Talking the matter over with an experienced Christian worker, she was advised to expect God to move in her husband's life. Mr Miles was responsible for a stretch of line that included Mersham Tunnel which is one mile, 352 yards long. One evening, whilst George Jeffreys' meetings were taking place, Mr Miles was walking through the tunnel when he clearly heard a voice behind him call out, 'Repent, for the Kingdom of heaven is at hand'. Stunned and shaken, he turned to see who was speaking, but there was no one there. He knew that God was speaking to him. He finished his job and went home but said nothing to anyone. During the evening meal he sat in silence, for, contrary to custom, he had changed into his best suit, a thing he rarely did on a weeknight. His son tells us what happened next:

> 'Mother broke the silence, saying, "Are you going to the meeting tonight, Dad?" I immediately thought, Oh dear, mother has done it again; there will be another row. But,

to my utter astonishment, father replied in a most subdued manner, "Yes I'm coming with you tonight." I couldn't believe my own ears.'

They arrived at the meeting: the son takes up the story again:

'We were singing the second hymn, "Send the light, the blessed gospel light", when father, like Saul of Tarsus, was smitten to the floor by the power of God. The little meeting was disturbed. Someone was hurrying for a glass of water, I remember being frightened, but George Jeffreys knew exactly what was taking place. With an authoritative voice charged with the power of the Holy Ghost, he commanded, "Leave that man alone, God is dealing with him".

We were all reassured and had a profound sense of God's over-ruling presence and purpose. All fear was removed for God had the matter in hand. After a little while my father got up from the floor, his face radiant with the glory of God. It was obvious that he had been 'delivered from the power of darkness and translated into the kingdom of God's dear son' . . . The Revival meetings were set ablaze with the fire of God. My father was born again. I shall never forget the dynamic change that came in our home that night; a change that was to abide throughout his earthly pilgrimage.

Father had been a keen card player. Several packs of cards always adorned our mantle-shelf, but on arriving home that glorious night, father's first act was to throw them all on the fire. The preacher had said no word about smoking, but God was working so mightily in my father's life that he proceeded to take all his pipes, the pipe rack and tobacco and consigned them to the flames . . . In the larder was a barrel of home made wine, fairly potent stuff. The one time precious liquid was allowed to run down the drain, after which the barrel was destroyed that it might have no further part in our new home . . . Having put away for ever the unholy things of the old life, father took the precious, holy word of God and instituted the family altar in his home by reading from the sacred page. Mother led us in prayer, praise and thanksgiving.'

George returned to Ireland once more, where, apart from occasional visits to England, he was to concentrate most of his efforts during the next five years. It was to be in Ireland that he became pastor of a settled congregation for the first and only time in his life. Stephen remained as the minister of Island Place, Llanelly, during the same period.

6: The Band of Brothers

On his return to Ireland at the end of 1914, George made contact with a few of the small groups of Pentecostals living there. There were small groups meeting in Belfast and in Bangor. Some could trace their beginnings to the early part of 1908, but their numbers were very small and they made little impact upon the city of Belfast.

George had begun preaching at the Christmas Convention, Dover Street where he met a group of young men. Following the Convention he was invited to meet a few of them in Monaghan on Thursday, January 7th, 1915. There were seven in the group who met in Knox's Temperance Hotel. The purpose of the meeting, as recorded in the Minute Book of the Elim Evangelistic Band, was that they, 'came together for the purpose of discussing the best means of reaching Ireland with the Full Gospel on Pentecostal Lines'. They concluded that:

> 'George Jeffreys, of South Wales, who was present with us, be invited to take up a permanent evangelistic work in Ireland and that a centre be chosen by him for the purpose of establishing a church out of which evangelists would be sent into towns and villages, and that a tent be hired, for the purpose of holding a Gospel Mission during the month of July to commence the work in Ireland.'

At the second meeting, held in July in the home of Jack Wilkinson of North Road, Monaghan, it was reported that George Jeffreys was to hold meetings in a tent in North Road, Monaghan. At the same meeting it was also reported that two workers had agreed to join the Evangelistic Band. These were Robert Ernest Darragh, a former Preston student from Bangor and Margaret Montgomery Streight, also of Bangor. It is interesting to note that Margaret Streight had applied to the Pentecostal Missionary Union a few years before but had been rejected as being 'too fanatical'. (A few years later she married Robert Mercer, another member of the Evangelistic Band. She died in March 1962).

During July and August, 1915, William Gillespie and Robert Darragh endeavoured to establish a centre in Belfast. As a result of their efforts they managed to find a disused laundry in Hunter Street, Donegal Road, and this was rented as a Mission. George Jeffreys was asked to hold meetings there and the building was secured on a three year lease, William Gillespie and George Jeffreys being the named tenants. Two men stood as surety for the place and George Jeffreys was invited to accept the pastorate.

George was asked to compile a booklet containing the doctrines that were to be proclaimed by the church, which was given the name, 'Elim Christ Church'. The statement of faith, *What We Believe*, makes it clear that they were contending for the faith which was once delivered to the saints. They believed that such faith should be contended for in every age. They believed that at the time much of this was being denied by religious leaders. They regarded themselves as a spiritual movement similar in style to others that had arisen from time to time in the history of the Christian Church. They further stated that, 'We can expect the onslaught of the enemy to be furious, in his seeking to counterfeit and to produce extravagance, which we must be careful to avoid, by continuing steadfastly in God's precious word'. The brethren agreed to accept this statement of faith and they also agreed, 'that no member of any other assembly be asked to join the church'.

It is clear that they had no intention of establishing a new denomination. It was their desire to be an evangelistic agency with the express purpose of reaching out into a needy district where they sought to win people to Christ. The measure of their success can be judged by the fact that by October, 1917 it was necessary for them to seriously consider obtaining more suitable premises, 'as the present building had become too small to accommodate the people that came'.

A disused church building in Melbourne Street, Belfast was secured and it became the second of more than twenty buildings that were obtained in Ireland by 1920. It was a considerable improvement on the old Hunter Street building. That place was described by Frederick Farlow, who was one of the group who first met George Jeffreys in Monaghan:

> 'The surroundings are anything but beautiful, in fact it is situated in one of the worst streets in the city, the name of which had to be changed several times, owing to the sinfulness of its inhabitants. Outside the entrance door there is lamp-standard without a whole pane of glass, and the children of the street have turned this into a Maypole, so those coming to worship have difficulty in entering the building. To look at the building from the outside it seems as if there has been a battle in the street and the building had come in for the worst of the conflict. There is not a whole pane of glass in any of the windows. To put new glass in these windows would cost too much, so we decided to fill the openings with some old rags, so Principal (George Jeffreys) with some other willing workers got busy at the job. Before the building was converted into an Elim Mission Hall it was used as a laundry, and all around the walls were to be seen pieces of old machinery.'

They gave the place the name Elim for two reasons. In the first place it was called after the Elim Mission, Lytham, Lancashire, where George had preached on a number of occasions during the time when he was a student at the nearby Preston Bible School. The name Elim was also a biblical name. It was the name given to an oasis in the desert where the children of Israel found refreshment soon after they left Egypt on their journey to the Promised Land (Exodus 15:27). In Wales, it was common practice for individual churches to have biblical names, Siloh, Carmel, Bethel, Ebenezer and Elim could be found in every valley. George had told Henry Morgidge, founder and builder of the Lytham Elim Mission that if he built a church he would call it Elim: that was just what he did. It is probable that the second meeting place might have been called Ebenezer after a place in Maesteg or one in Plymouth. The name Elim proved popular, so it was retained.

A number of young men joined the Evangelistic Band. Former Preston students E.J. Phillips and Ernie Darragh, from Birmingham John Carter, later to be the General-Secretary of the Assemblies of God, and T.J. Jones, later to be a noted teacher in the American Assemblies of God Bible School; E.W. Hare, former President of Cambridge University Christian Union and Cyril Taylor, a final year medical student who would be their first missionary, being ordained in April 1920 for service in the Belgian Congo.

The members of the Evangelistic Band were all 'on faith lines', which meant that they shared any money and goods that were given to them. Times were very hard but the work continued to grow. George Jeffreys was frequently absent from Ireland as he accepted appointments to conduct meetings in many places on the mainland.

At this time, when money was very short, they received news of a sudden, and unexpected windfall. In Wales, a certain lady who had got to know George Jeffreys after he had spoken at Convention meeting in Bracknall and Hereford, died rather suddenly on November 5th, 1917. When the contents of her will became known it was discovered that Mrs Jane Rees had made George Jeffreys, 'residuary legatee of all that may remain of the estate after payment of all debts and legacies'. The possibility of receiving a considerable sum from the estate that was said to be worth over £5,000 (today's value would be more than

£100,000) was a prospect that would have been more than useful at a time when every penny had to be carefully counted. As time went on, however, the matter became more complicated and the will was contested by several different people. The matter was eventually settled in September 1925, but not before the legal costs had amounted to more than a thousand pounds. The final amount that George Jeffreys received was almost a thousand pounds and this was used to pay off the money owing on one of the Irish churches.

As the money was left to George Jeffreys, the court advised that it would be better if it was given to him as a representative of a charitable or missionary enterprise. It was on this directive from the court and the advice of John Leech K.C. of Dublin that a property holding body was formed. They took the name of the 'Elim Pentecostal Alliance Council'. Thus, what had started as a simple evangelistic effort by a small group anxious to win others for Christ now became a separate denomination.

With the outbreak of World War 1, evangelistic activity had to be curtailed. As a pastor of the Elim Christ Church, Belfast, George Jeffreys was granted exemption from military service when general mobilisation came into force in 1916. John Leech K.C. became President of the Council. Stephen also became a member, though he remained in Llanelly. A Church of Ireland clergyman, Thomas Hackett of Bray, brother of the Primate of all Ireland, became an advisor.

7: Opposition and Opportunity

Both Stephen and George found a ready response to their ministry on the mainland. They were well accepted as preachers by inter-denominational groups. It was one such gathering at Sion College, London, that George gave a personal testimony at a meeting of the Prophetical Society. At the end of May, in the following year, 1921, Stephen held Revival meetings at Sion College. This was prior to the opening of their forty-ninth Conference.

Towards the end of 1921 Stephen held meetings in Horbury Chapel, Kensington, for the minister, F.W. Pitt. A young Pentecostal pastor from Edinburgh named Donald Gee was asked to play the piano for the meetings which went on for several weeks. There were a large number of conversions and many cases of healing that drew the attention of the press. It was arranged that Stephen would return for further meetings in July 1922 and an agreement was drawn up in which it was proposed that Stephen should become associate pastor of Horbury Chapel along with Mr Pitt. In the event of Mr Pitt retiring, or on his death, Stephen was to become the sole minister. As things turned out matters were to be very different.

Such was the anticipation for Stephen's second visit to Horbury Chapel that they spent £250 on renovations to the chapel. Relations between the minister and Stephen were very good and Mr Pitt asked if, in the meantime, he could help in Stephen's meetings in Clapham. Then, suddenly and unexpectedly Mr Pitt wrote an article in the magazine, *Prophetic News and Israel's Messenger* in which he bitterly attacked the Pentecostals in general and speaking in tongues in particular. He described it passionately:

> 'The movement is consecration gone off the rails . . . most of the inspiration is emotional . . . its development . . . is a history of shame . . . excesses of Pentecostalists open the door to immorality. They mistake hysterics for the baptism of the Holy Ghost . . . groups of men and women roll about the floor in a frenzy, clutching at each other, howling, and leering.'

It was not to be wondered that Stephen was deeply shocked and hurt by such intemperate language in a Christian magazine which had so recently printed some of his sermons. As a consequence he withdrew from the proposed mission at Horbury Chapel. Mr Pitt was very annoyed and threatened him with legal action in an effort to recover the money they had spent in anticipation of the expected success of Stephen's visit.

In January Mr Pitt had written to Stephen in the most friendly terms. He was delighted that many of the converts of the 1921 mission were coming to the meetings. The next letter in July was decidely hostile. The opening, 'My dear friend', and the closing, 'With love in the Lord Jesus. Yours for Victory', was replaced by the cool, 'Dear Mr Jeffreys'. After the threats, a cooler, 'Yours sincerely'.

Stephen did not reply right away. (he never was a very good letter writer) but eventually he wrote (with the help and advice of friends) what was for him a lengthy answer. He expressed his surprise and deep regret as well as his, 'deep sense of pain' at Mr Pitt's remarks about the Pentecostals. He expected such remarks from worldlings, but at Horbury he thought he was in the house of friends. He went on to declare:

> 'You listened to my preaching for many weeks; you heard my testimony on the Holy Ghost baptism with signs following, old and young speaking in tongues, which had marked my ministry for so many years . . . You never

raised your voice against anything but encouraged the work.'

After quoting some of the strong language of the article, Stephen went on to ask:

'But Mr Pitt did you imagine all this would affect me? I am heart and soul with you in condemning excesses; there are excesses in every branch of Christian service, in every community of believers – the papers for example frequently contain terrible stories of licentious clergy and immoral ministers, yet you have not confined yourself to denouncing excesses; you condemn in sweeping language people who believe in the baptism of the Holy Spirit and speak in tongues . . . I am a simple man and all I have is my love for my Lord and the strength he gives me to carry out the Great Commission, but I warn you Mr Pitt that I have seen ministers as learned and clever as you being dealt with in a terrible manner for playing lightly with the work of the Holy Spirit and attributing to emotion and demonism the experience wrought in them by the mighty power of God . . . One thing is certain now, the door of Horbury has been closed to me forever by your hand.'

The newspapers of the time confirm that miracles of healing occured in the meetings in Horbury Chapel in October 1921. The same papers also testify to the fact that speaking in tongues was also a feature of the meetings. They were reported in the papers, from the *Yorkshire Post* to *Thomson's Weekly News* and many more. Mr Pitt's claimed ignorance of such things is strange indeed. It gives us no joy, but should cause no surprise either to record that Horbury Chapel went into a serious decline not long after that time and eventually it had to be closed. It is worth noting that when the empty building came on to the market in 1930 it was purchased by George Jeffreys. Better known today as Kensington Temple, it is the leading Elim Church in London with a regular congregation that numbers over a thousand.

The opposition of Mr Pitt was part of a concerted attack on Pentecostalism that manifested itself in several places. The previously open attitude, which enabled Stephen to minister in many churches no longer operated, and the brothers found themselves increasingly drawn to independent Pentecostal Missions.

In March 1922 Dr Ernest Goode, Secretary to the Prophetical Society at whose meetings both George and Stephen had preached in 1920, wrote to Stephen to tell him that there was a lot of trouble over them being announced as speakers for the forthcoming meetings in London. He named several Christian leaders who were refusing to take part in the meetings if the brothers spoke. As a result the proprietor of the *Christian Herald* dropped the names of the complaining ministers and the brothers from the list of speakers. He told Dr Goode privately that he thought that the brothers should take part in the meetings unannounced!

Stephen spent three months in Grimsby from the beginning of January to the end of March 1922. His brother George followed on at the end of that period. The brothers had worked together in their first mission but for some time they had begun to develop their own individuality. There was no rift between them at this stage, but there was a very clear difference between the two brothers. The difference was to become so marked that even some of those who knew them very well in later years thought that they were step-brothers.

In Grimsby, the local Methodist minister wrote a description of George's visit to the town. He spoke of the anticipation of the people as they awaited the arrival of George when he came to take Stephen's place after he left the town on March 31st:

'What', they asked, 'will his brother be like?' Those who were expecting another Pastor Stephen would be disappointed, for never were two brothers so different, in features, in mannerisms and method.

Three years later, Agnes Adams described Stephen as '. . . a little below average height, broad shouldered, auburn haired. His features are well modelled and pleasing, but the chief charm of his face is its expression. He carries the glory that we see in the eyes of happy lovers . . . One sees him without knowing that he is in love with every human soul. He seems to stretch out his arms to every being God made, and love it.'

No doubt there are many different Welshmen, but anyone who has spent some time amongst them will clearly recognise two distinct types. The first is the older working miner, hard working but essentially simple in outlook. He is perhaps more at home by the fireside without a collar and tie and amongst friends. He feels ill at ease in more genteel and polite company. Stephen was one of this sort.

George, on the other hand was different, though shy and retiring, he would not have been out of place in a drawing room. His carefully chosen words were delivered in a rich baritone voice, whether to a small, intimate gathering or to a crowd of several thousand. At times his words could be so compelling that a leading London newspaper hoarding carried the caption, 'London Audience Mesmerized'. George was careful in all his work, appointments were kept and letters answered. Every detail of planning was properly arranged. After a few years he was able to have a personal secretary and campaign manager. They would meet the press, book the halls, arrange advance publicity and posters.

Stephen found such details irksome. It was not uncommon to find that he had agreed to be in several places at the same time. On more than one occasion he would be unable to be present for a series of meetings as he had promised to speak at the meeting of a friend some miles away, so a substitute speaker had to be found, often at the last minute. His friends would tell him how they proposed to run the meetings and they would suggest the order of the programme, when the collection would be taken, who would give the announcements and other important details. Once Stephen was preaching, he would be so carried away that the agreed order would be forgotten. It was great for his hearers, but to his friends waiting in the wings or sitting behind him on the platform things were viewed in a far different way. Yet you could not take offence at anything he did. It was all done with an openess and honesty born of a simple, child-like faith, void of offence.

The active opposition from religious leaders and a growing response from a large number of ordinary men and women who came in increasing numbers to their meetings gave a new direction to the brothers' work. This work became, in both cases, increasingly to be directed into two groups which emerged to form the two main groups within British Pentecostalism; Elim and the Assemblies of God. How these groups were formed and a little of their development and the part that the brothers played in this will make our next chapter.

8: From Mission to Denominations

In the years between 1908 and 1914, there was a considerable growth in the number of people who were in sympathy with, or who claimed a personal experience of Pentecostalism. A few of these were ministers in the denominations but not many of them were persons of position or influence. The main area from which support began to emerge was amongst a number of laymen who were leaders of small, independent mission halls. Such mission halls could be found in London (where there were more than a dozen); in the Birmingham area (where there were three), and in a variety of places around the country, including Manchester, Leeds, Plymouth, Lytham, Preston and Bournemouth. Up to 1914 many of the people found their way to the Sunderland Convention but with the outbreak of the First World War the work suffered a considerable setback. In the first place convention meetings were no longer possible. War work, conscription or conscientious objection claimed a large number of the younger men and there was a break in the continuity of the emerging fellowship. Contacts that were so essential to the infant movement had to be suspended. Before the war there was only one clearly defined group – the Apostolic Faith work of W. O. Hutchinson in Bournemouth dating from 1908. All the rest existed in unconnected missions.

George Jeffreys started the Elim Evangelistic Band in Belfast in January 1915. In the following year a large number of the Apostolic Churches that had been part of the Bournemouth group branched out on their own under the leadership of Dan P. Williams and his brother W.J. Williams. These became the Apostolic Church and at first they were found mainly in Wales. In Scotland, the Burning Bush Assembly of Andrew Turnbull joined up with the Williams' work after the end of the war. In July, 1917, George Jeffreys was 'ordained' by his brother Stephen and the Welsh speaking minister, W Moelfren Morgan from Ammanford who was preaching at the Evangelistic Band Convention in Ireland at the time.

Several attempts were made between 1922 and 1926 to bring together those groups to form a single unit but all the efforts were to no avail. There was fear on the part of some that the powerful personality of George Jeffreys would dominate the group. Some were very fearful of 'Authority' that sought to stifle freedom. As a result there emerged three main groups, Elim, Apostolic and from 1924, the Assemblies of God. Apart from the work in Dowlais where Stephen was pastor, the first Elim work in mainland Britain was at Leigh-on-Sea, Essex. After difficulties were encountered in the Apostolic Faith work, George conducted a series of meetings, first in a drawing room and later in a newly built Mission Hall. In October, 1921 George Kingston, a local business man was ordained as pastor.

In the north, a former Salvation Army officer and 'Apostle' in Hutchinson's Bournemouth work, Ernest Boulton, had been leading a small work in May Street, Hull. George Jeffreys had met him at the Unity Conference in Sheffield in 1922 when Boulton had been secretary. After the failure of these efforts towards unity, instigated by former Preston student William Burton, home from the Congo, George Jeffreys accepted the invitation to go to Hull. The meetings were a great success and E.C.W. Boulton joined the Elim work shortly after that time. He would eventually hold high office in Elim.

In 1922 the administration of the Elim work was transferred from Belfast to London where, in Clapham, George and Stephen had been holding meetings. A former Methodist Church in Park Crescent was purchased together with a piece of ground next door. The building was used as a meeting place for the first Elim Church in London and the offices were transferred to the same site. Eventually a two storey building was erected (later a third floor was added) to house the printing press and the Elim Publishing Company. (This was the beginning of what was to be called Victory Press, later to be absorbed into Kingsway Publications.) A lot of time was given to consolidating the work at Clapham and a proposed visit to the United States had to be delayed.

In 1923 meetings were held in Tamworth, Ashborne and Letchworth, mainly for the friends and family of members of the Evangelistic Band. In each place the small witness was encouraged and converts added. One member of the Band, John Carter, left Ireland to help his brother Howard, who had taken over the pastorate of an assembly at Lee, where George and Stephen had successful meetings in 1920. Howard also started a Bible School in Hampstead for a few students. Both Howard and John Carter were to take a leading part in the formation of the Assemblies of God in 1924.

After a meeting in Aston, Birmingham on February 1st, 1924 and further meetings in Highbury, London, early in May, a group of some three dozen churches from England, one from Ireland and forty from Wales, joined together to form the Assemblies of God of Great Britain and Ireland. The Elim group were not invited to the meeting at Highbury, but when they heard about them they wrote to the assembled brethren and asked if it was possible for them to '. . . get together to talk over the matter of uniting for the sake and glory of God'. They expressed the desire to contribute, if possible, to the uniting of the body of Pentecostal believers in the land. They also stated that it was their desire, '. . . to prevent (if successful) a breach coming between yourselves as Assemblies of God and the work of the Elim Pentecostal Alliance'.

Three of the Elim Overseers went to the conference on the last day where they made a considerable impact. Even though much of the ground had been covered on the first day, and the assembled brethren had gone so far as to divide up leadership positions amongst themselves, E.J. Phillips made the startling suggestion that the Elim group should become the evangelistic section of the new body and that they should unite. It was a bold sugestion, perhaps it was too bold for that time because the matter was left in the air without a final decision being made but senior brethren agreed to have further meetings.

The date of the proposed visit to the United States and Canada was settled and a party of five sailed from Southampton on the *Empress of Scotland* June 21st, 1924. The party consisted of George and Stephen Jeffreys, R.E. Darragh, E.C.W. Boulton and James McWhirter. They travelled together for some 15,000 miles and they were away until the middle of October.

The absence of so many leading men at such a time seriously affected the possibilities of the link being forged between the two groups. The visit also helped to convince George Jeffreys that it would be better for him to remain apart from the new group. Writing to E.J. Phillips from San Jose, California on August 25th 1924 he advised that:

> 'The further I go in this Pentecostal Movement the more convinced I am that the democratic way of doing things is wrong. I am still persuaded that nothing will hinder me from going on with the Alliance as an independent work. Subject of course to the coming Band meeting. Don't have a single thing to do with them until we can meet to discuss the whole situation.'

From the same place he writes on September 11th:

> 'The Assemblies of God is not working here. I am still determined not to join them in Britain.'

In Britain it was the application by a group of Welsh Pentecostal Assemblies to join the American Assemblies of God that had precipitated the formation of the British group in February and May 1924. Yet no direct link between the British and American groups was forged. At that time the American group was going through a hard patch and though they were only ten years old, they had suffered a major split on doctrinal grounds and their total membership was under 50,000.

When the Evangelistic Band finally met in Belfast in December, 1924 they considered the question of amalgamation with the Assemblies of God of Great Britain and Ireland and passed the following resolution:

> 'We, having beforehand carefully examined the minutes and prayerfully considered the question of amalgamation with the Assemblies of God of Great Britain and Ireland, believe it to be the will of God that we work each on our own lines, both striving, side by side with mutual sympathy, for the salvation of souls and for the truths which are dear to us.'

Thus, two seperate groups were created. The difference between them was that the Assemblies of God in the U.K. were congregational in their form of government, while Elim had a central administration, more akin at first to the Salvation Army (without the structure of rank or uniform) but later, much nearer to that of the Methodist Church, with Conference and Districts.

9: The Parting of the Ways

No one really wanted to organise Stephen, but someone had to try. He was a glorious man, you could not help but love him, but his sheer simplicity and openess could be, and was abused. He tried to share himself with everyone. There were just not enough hours in the day for him to do all the things he wanted to do. There were not enough days in his diary (if he ever kept one) and his friends tried so hard to help. He would forget everything when he was preaching, announcements, collection and directions to converts all went by the board. The periods as pastor, for seven years in Llanelly, five years in Dowlais and a short time in Southend were great times, but considering his frequent absence, they must also have been frustrating times for the leaders there. He finally bade farewell to Dowlais on November 2nd, 1924 and joined his brother as a full-time evangelist. A few days later he was conducting meetings in Stonehouse Town Hall, Plymouth.

The early part of 1925 saw a real opening for the brothers as they returned to London once more. The fame and expectancy of 1913 had been short-lived, cut short by the outbreak of the war. Building up the work at Clapham had not been easy, but at the end of two and a half years of hard work they had a church that cost £4,500 with only £900 owing and a regular congregation approaching 500. One of their regular Clapham members travelled in each Sunday from Barking, Essex. Mr Thorn asked them if they would hold meetings there as he was finding it difficult coming all that way every Sunday, even though Clapham Common was by that time linked to the Underground. Stephen accepted the request and opened in Barking on Sunday,

January 18th 1925 to a small group who met in the Public Baths. A young man fron Wales, William Llewellyn Bell, recently qualified as a teacher, joined Stephen. He played the piano, sang and generally assisted in the meetings. Only a few people came to the first service and the next meeting was not much better attended. As well as evening meetings, they decided to hold special services on some afternoons when they prayed for the sick. These meetings were to be held on Tuesday, Wednesday and Thursday. At the first of these meetings there was only a small gathering. The people were requested to form a line and they were asked to come up to the platform where the evangelist would lay hands upon them and pray. The first person was prayed for, but nothing appeared to happen. After that a man stood waiting his turn. Nearly sixty years later, the eyes of retired headmaster Willie Bell would light up with excitement as he told the story once more. He had noticed the man when they were on their way to the meeting that afternoon. He was obviously in great need. Walking with great difficulty and only with the aid of crutches he dragged his helpless limbs along. Now he stood there on the simple, raised platform in front of the evangelist. Stephen made no fuss, as in the most simple manner, he put his hands on the man's head and prayed. Immediately Tom English felt a strange sensation; it was as if his helpless lower limbs had been connected to some power source. He felt a strange sensation as new life and feeling returned. He laid aside his crutches and with the sudden surge of new power he found that he was not only able to stand up but he could walk, run and jump. With a cry he jumped off the platform, ran up the aisle and out into the street. On his lips was the excited cry, 'I'm healed!' This caused considerable excitement amongst the small group of people at the meeting that afternoon. From that time on the only problem about the numbers was finding enough room for everyone.

Tom English was not the only person healed that day. A little five year old girl who had never walked was brought to the meeting by her parents. As they brought her out for prayer, Stephen lifted her in his arms. He wept as he prayed, 'Jesus, look at this little girl, you have given her legs, and you intend her to walk. In the name of Jesus I'm going to put you down. WALK! My Jesus will never let you down.' Walk she did. The parents were deeply moved and were converted.

Living in St. Awdry's Road, the same road as the little girl's family, were Mr and Mrs Coulson, whose teenage son, Ernest was unable to walk: he was confined to a dreadful spinal carriage. When his mother heard of the healing of the little girl she asked her husband if she could take Ernest. Her husband, a retired army officer, said,'No'. Undeterred, Mrs Coulson took Ernest along to the meeting and he was healed. When Mr Coulson returned home that night his son was standing at the gate, perfectly cured. The father's reaction was far from favourable. He turned his wife and son out of the house. After they had spent the night with neighbours, he permitted them to return home and after a time he too went to the meetings. He was eventually converted and subsequently became a member and served as an officer in the church that was formed as a result of the crusade. The Barking Crusade proved to be a turning point in the history of the Elim Movement as well as in the lives of the two brothers.

Ernest Boulton, in his book, *George Jeffreys – A Ministry of the Miraculous* (1928), tells of the beginning of the Barking meetings, 'Pastor Stephen Jeffreys, was appointed to conduct.' He offers no explanation for these words (though at the time that the book was written Stephen was no longer working with his brother). The book does not explain the subsequent disappearance of Stephen from the narrative.

During the time that the Elim delegation were in Canada and the United States (when Boulton was with them), it was agreed that Stephen should become more fully linked with the Elim work. He had been listed as a member of the Elim Pentecostal Alliance Council in the first edition of the *Elim*

Evangel, dated December 1919. There is no record of him ever being ordained as a member of the Band. He was granted honorary credentials with the Pentecostal Assemblies of Canada for the duration of their visit (this enabled the holder to a discount when travelling by train). The doubt about dates as far as his ordination was concerned is typical of Stephen's casual approach to such matters.

George agreed that Elim should become responsible for Stephen. In an endeavour to set this on a proper basis an agreeement was drawn up. A group named the Full Gospel Forward Movement Council was formed. The three members were E. C.W. Boulton, E. J. Phillips and a business man, Ludwig Naumann of the Baltic Exchange. Signed on June 18th, 1925, the Agreement read as follows:

> 'Pastor Stephen Jeffreys agrees to devote his full time to conducting the missions or other appointments arranged for him by the said Council, to preach the full Gospel . . . For this he shall receive a salary of Five Pounds (£5) per week, in addition to being allowed all necessary travelling expenses and the occupation of the house free from rent, rates, or taxes . . .
> (4) In consideration of the above, all collections and offerings at all missions, together with all private gifts whatsoever to Pastor Stephen Jeffreys or his wife are to be put to the funds of the Full Gospel Forward Movement Council.
> All correspondence addressed to Pastor Jeffreys to be opened by the said Council.
> (5) This agreement may be terminated by three calendar months' notice being given on any date by either party thereto . . .'

Stephen sold his house in Merthyr Tydfil for £600 and moved, with his wife and his son Edward, to Leigh-on-Sea, Essex where he bought a bungalow for £1,300. A group of men, including George Kingston, pastor of Leigh-on-Sea, purchased a piece of land at Southend for £720 where they planned to erect a building costing £2,000.

The Barking meetings ended for Stephen on February 15th and the next week he proceeded to Hendon and afterwards to follow up at Forest Hill, where Mr Darragh and Miss Adams had been struggling for some weeks. He had been asked to conduct his first mission under the new arrangements but on June 20th, two days after signing the agreement, he wrote to E. J. Phillips to say that he was, 'feeling unable to take another large mission on during the hot months'. He asked to carry on at Surrey Tabernacle (a large former Baptist Church in Wansley Street, Walworth Road) for some meetings. We find him spending a few days at Pontypridd in Wales during his holidays in September:

> 'I am now packed out, the place is suffocating, hundreds outside, I cannot get a larger place. I could command a congregation of 3,000, but I am handicapped, there is a wonderful place here, I am roasted with heat and will be obliged to close next Thursday – to take a rest before I commence at Notting Hill Gate. The same congregation is rushing back to the meeting . . . If I could have a building I could make money, and I feel already worked out. It is awful to preach in such a hot atmosphere. There will be a good work established.'

The meetings in Notting Hill Gate were to fulfil a promise to Ben Griffiths, of Peniel Chapel.

Stephen then went on to Margate in November where he held meetings for George Every, a former member of the Elim Evangelistic Band. By this time it became increasingly clear that the brothers were developing ministries along different lines. Part of this was because their temperaments were so different. A measure of the blame must be placed at the door of those who were prepared to put ideas into Stephen's mind that prejudiced him against his brother and caused him to suspect George of less than worthy motives.

Stephen could sometimes be very unwise in the things

that he said and did. On one occasion he was preaching at Grimsby when he spotted some well-dressed ladies in the congregation. He made a few pointed remarks about how hard it was for the rich to enter into heaven. One of the ladies was deeply hurt, she was not that wealthy but she had loaned Elim a sum of money when she has sold a property and later on she was to lend the money to purchase the Bible College at Clapham. She was so upset by what Stephen had said that she wrote to his brother and asked for her money back. It needed all of brother George's tact to save the situation. Stephen thought that his brother was jealous of his success, and he said so. It was a sad episode and though efforts were made to patch things up relations were strained for a time. It did not help when Stephen later worked in areas very close to the places where his brother's churches had been established.

In October 1929 the feelings between the brothers had so deteriorated that George found it necessary to write to the churches in the East End of London, (East Ham, Ilford, Canning Town and Barking):

> 'Pastor Stephen by coming into your midst has broken a solemn vow . . . he has also made charges of a serious nature against myself personally, and also against the Elim work . . . I have had to meet these accusations in nearly every place I have ministered throughout the country.
>
> It is his avowed intention to open up churches close to our own, and such action must inevitably result in splitting of Elim Churches, which I know you will deeply deplore.
>
> Little did I think when I booked the Baths Hall, Barking in 1924 (sic) and engaged my brother, Pastor Stephen, as the evangelist to run the Elim campaign, that I should be called upon in 1929 to refute such misrepresentations of our work.'

The brothers were to be reconciled, but Stephen's later

years left him somewhat incapacitated and he rarely preached. This did not prevent George from putting forward his brother's name to the Executive Council at their meeting in May, 1938 when he suggested that Stephen should take over the pastorate of the Swansea Church. The Council did not feel that such a proposal was really workable. In any case Stephen's health at the time would hardly have made this a sensible proposition.

10: Evangelist at Large

When Stephen left Elim in 1926 he was free to accept preaching engagements from wherever they came. In the period immediately after the First World War, there had been invitations from Methodist and Baptist Churches as well as from groups of churches, particularly in Wales. Now however, most of these had dried up. It was from many of the small Pentecostal groups that the invitations now came. Many of these struggling groups looked to Stephen to bring them the increased numbers they desperately needed. In some cases the crowds who flocked to their meetings overwhelmed their limited resources. Some of them were able to build up and sustain very good churches as a result. Several of these were to become leading churches in the newly formed Assemblies of God.

He was in Plaistow, London, in January, Ramsgate in February and Hackney in March, Dover was visited in April, and Walthamstow at the beginning of May. At the end of the month, he was in Bedford where the Corn Exchange had been hired. Bedford had many interesting Pentecostal connections: it was the home of Cecil Polhill, squire of Howbury Hall; Costain Street Mission had been pastored by Robert Jardine, later to achieve notoriety when, as an Anglican minister, he officiated at the ceremony when Edward VIII married Mrs Simpson. Bedford was also the home of the Phillips family who were to give Elim the three brothers, known by their initials of E.J., F.B., and H.C.

At the end of August, Donald Gee invited Stephen to visit Edinburgh where he spent fifteen days. The Scots did not respond as quickly to Stephen as they did to his brother, but a good impression was made, and it helped by adding a few to the assembly on his brief, single mission, north of the Border. This was followed by a brief return to Tumble in West Wales. He returned to Kent and was in Margate for the first two weeks in November. This was followed by meetings in Chelmsford.

In the following year (1927) his meetings reached their high peak as he went from Folkestone in January and on to Canterbury in February. In March and early April he moved north to Bishop Auckland, where, during a period of six weeks, the whole community was stirred. In that time, there were hundreds of conversions and numerous cases of healing. Amongst the converts were four brothers, Norman, Clarence, Harold and Clyde Young, all of whom became ministers in the Assemblies of God.

To select two cases of healing is almost arbitary: thirteen year old Celia May Brown from Newcastle on Tyne was born blind. Her healing, which began on March 11th, is related by Rev J. W. Adams, Vicar of Wall, Lichfield, who attended many of Stephen's meetings and wrote a book about his experiences. Telling Celia's story he says:

> 'She did not then appear to have any eyes, even in embryo condition, and had never known the difference between light and dark, day or night. Immediately after the laying on of hands a new world began to be opened for her. With her new and very small eyes she discerned the very marked difference between light and shade. The next day she saw more clearly, and soon she was able to count and pick up pennies from a white tablecloth.'

That is how Stephen told the story to the vicar who published it later that year. The vicar met Celia and talked with her on several occasions and testified that she was able to count fingers that were held up before her. She had blue eyes like those of her father.

Two weeks later, on Saturday, March 26th a young woman from the village of Evenwood, a few miles south east of Bishop Auckland, was brought to the meeting by colliery ambulance. She had been sick for two years and eight months and had not left her bedroom in all that time. She had to be lifted from her bed and she was fed through a feeding cup. She had lost her voice and would sometimes cough uncontrollably for three or four hours. Her face was covered with a terrible scab that had formed round her mouth and which would not heal. Her sister,Margaret, had been to the meeting and came back with a glowing report. Their mother and a Mr Pasey, a Pentecostal man from the village, arranged for her to go to the meeting. They carried her on a stretcher into the meeting and left her at the foot of the stairs outside the hall. The pastor was sent for and when he came, he paused half way down the stairs, looking at her with great compassion on his face, he asked her sister what was the matter. She tried to explain, but words failed her. Turning to Nellie, he asked, 'Do you love Jesus?' As she was unable to speak, she simply nodded her head. 'And do you believe that Jesus can heal you?' he asked. Nellie nodded once more. Quietly the pastor declared, 'Yes, He will'. With these words, he came to where they had left her, and kneeling on the muddy floor, he began to pray. There was so much wrong with her, she lay wrapped in blankets and a coat around her with a hot water bottle to keep her warm; unable to speak but with her mouth open all the time; deaf in her left ear and with a crooked right arm and heavily bandaged knees. Stephen laid hands on her and prayed. Her sister heard him say, 'Can you walk?' To her astonishment she heard her sister reply in a weak voice, 'Thank God, I can talk – and I can walk.' With that she put aside the heavy hot water bottle, took two steps and then continued walking up and down the passage. Her sister, laughing and crying at the same time, picked her up in her arms and with a word from the pastor laid her back on the stretcher. The return journey home, especially when their mother came to the yard to meet them was memorable. Margaret was converted and great joy came into the home. Within an hour of returning home, the awful scab dropped from her lips. Another, similar place under one eye disappeared on the Sunday morning. Other marks on an arm and on her fingers, which had been there for two years, were gone by Tuesday. Her right arm that had been bent for thirteen years was straightened and her hearing was perfect. She subsequently became the leader of the Pentecostal Mission in the village and remained there for many years.

Meetings in Louth, Maidstone and Gravesend followed in the late spring and early summer, and in September Stephen began in Sunderland on the first Sunday in the month. The venue itself was an act of faith, the massive Victoria Hall, home of the Sunshine Brotherhood was the venue for the meetings. Alexander Boddy had retired by this time and was living at Pittington a few miles from Durham. None of the local clergy supported the meetings but ordinary people flocked there in vast numbers. Before long they formed queues around the hall and its capacity of 3,000 was insufficient to accommodate all who sought an entrance. The police had to be called to control the crowds who besieged the building. Numerically it was to be Stephen's greatest crusade. A local newspaper describing the many sick and afflicted who were brought there said that the hall was, 'resembling the scene in a waiting-room of a large hospital'. Not everyone was healed. Sometimes as many as 200 sick people were dealt with in a single day. On one day alone, six people were wheeled into the hall in carriages: they arose and walked, and left their carriages or wheeled them home themselves. According to a report in the *Bristol Times* in February, 1928, Stephen regarded the Sunderland meetings as his greatest. In the space of a month 3,362 converts were recorded. On one occasion a queue of over 1,000 were waiting outside at 8 p.m. to get into a meeting due to commence at 3 p.m. the next day.

Stephen stayed in the north for most of the remainder of the year, moving on to Spennymoor, Co. Durham where 1,362 converts were counted in two weeks. Chesterfield followed in October with 1,554 in three weeks. Bury added a further 2,042 in a three week period. At the end of the year he went to Manchester where John Nelson Parr, Chairman of the Assemblies of God and editor of *Redemption Tidings* had been labouring hard for some ten years. Parr had managed in that time to increase his assembly from seventeen to forty-five. At the time, it was the only Pentecostal Assembly in Manchester. As an act of faith they booked Leverhulme Town Hall for the campaign and the first meeting was on December 26th, 1927. Thousands of handbills were distributed in the area in near Arctic weather conditions. The Town Hall seated 600, but only about fifty people bothered to come. The first ten days were hopeless. However, in Nelson Parr's own words:

> 'God broke through after two weeks. One or two most amazing miracles took place then the crowds started coming . . . The last week of the campaign in Leverhulme Town Hall was a tremendous week of real Holy Ghost Revival. The meetings were crowded and miracles were taking place every night and many people accepting the Lord Jesus as their Saviour. Towards the end of the week we could not get the crowds into the hall.'

Nelson Parr wondered who was going to take over the meetings at the end of the campaign. He asked Stephen, 'Who shall we get to carry on this work after the campaign?' Stephen looked at him and said, 'You are the man'. With that he unselfishly asked Nelson Parr to preach one night and God blessed his message to the people. As a result, Parr resigned from his secure and responsible position at the Crossley factory, and became a full-time pastor. They continued to hold meetings in the Town Hall from January until the beginning of November, even though it cost them £15 per week in rent. A piece of ground was bought in Crowcroft Road, Longsight and on November 7th, 1928 Bethshan Tabernacle was opened. This became one of the largest Pentecostal churches in the United Kingdom. Nelson Parr stayed as pastor until his retirement in 1964.

Stephen moved on again, and later in January 1928 he was in Tunbridge Wells. On February 14th he was in Bristol where they hired the Y.M.C.A. Hall. Once again the same pattern was to be repeated. A small, slow start with support from a few of the faithful Pentecostals, then after a time, the numbers would grow. On a Sunday night some 1,300 were packed into the hall with hundreds turned away unable to find a seat. The larger Coulston Hall had to be hired to accommodate the crowds. Stephen's son, Edward went to Bristol with a friend who was to be inducted to the pastorate of the church there. When his friend saw the number of people who were there he realised that the task was too much for him and he backed out. He told Edward that he should take his place. Thus, Edward, who had helped his father in some of his meetings, now found himself in full-time ministry. Out of this he was to start the Bethel Evangelistic Society which had huge meetings, particularly in the Potteries and in Lancashire.

In May, Stephen went to Wakefield, after visits to Derby in March and Doncaster in April, where there were 1,100 converts recorded in two weeks.

On Whit Monday he was in Newcastle on Tyne. He met considerable opposition from the local press who opened their pages to a volume of correspondence from readers: the letters flew thick and fast. Stephen stayed aside from the fury, he never sought publicity, and in any case, he had previously made arrangements to leave for a tour overseas.

He left for several weeks in the United States and afterwards he went on to New Zealand and Australia. He arrived in New Zealand on October 22nd, accompanied by his wife, and with his nephew Tom Thomas, his sister Margaret Ann's son, as his song leader. They began in the new Exhibition Hall, Wellington, where they had a congregation of some 1,400. The numbers were to climb to 2,000, but later declined and they were transferred to the Pentecostal Church. Further meetings were held in New Plymouth, Palmerston North and Christchurch. Stephen preached at the Annual Conference of the New Zealand

Assemblies of God and then concluded his stay in the country with meetings in Auckland, leaving for Australia on February 22nd, 1929. The New Zealand papers were generally favourable in their reports of his meetings and helped to establish the Pentecostal work in the country.

The visit to Australia was a brief one with meetings in Richmond, a suburb of Melbourne, where there was an outstanding case of divine healing.

A newsvendor, well-known in the area, who had been deaf and dumb since the First World War was taken to the meeting by some of his 'friends', more as a cruel joke than with any serious intention. The power of God was present, however, and much to their surprise and his great delight, the man both heard and spoke. He ran down the aisle waving his arms and shouting, the people following him out into the road. Stephen turned to his nephew and said, 'there goes our congregation, Tom'. They came back at night, and so many came with them it was difficult to get near the church.

After holding meetings in Sydney, he sailed for South Africa where meetings were arranged by Archibald Cooper, who had been instrumental in bringing the various assemblies together leading to the formation of the British Assemblies of God in 1924. Meetings were held in Durban where black and white joined together in a large campaign held in a tent. From there they went on to Johanesburg where meetings were held in the City Hall. In spite of the difficulty of having to preach with interpreters translating his message into three or four languages, souls were saved, and there were many cases of healing. This was his first visit to South Africa, but he returned there after only a few months back in Britain. He was joined on the second visit by his nephew, Tom, and a fellow Welshman John Hewitt, who was converted through his ministry in Siloh Chapel, Nantyffyllon in 1915. John Hewitt had emigrated to Australia where he became pastor of Brisbane Assemblies of God.

When Stephen returned from South Africa he decided to

move to Ilford but later went back to Wales; first to Cardiff and later to Maesteg and Porthcawl. It was becoming apparent that there was a marked deterioration in his health. There had been years of constant meetings, sometimes for months on end with hardly a night off. Meetings were held in the afternoon and at night, sometimes going on to a late hour as more and more sick people pressed upon him for prayer. He just could not turn anyone away. He was often tired, and more than once he did not feel up to preaching (as for example in Sunderland) but when he found that a congregation was waiting to be ministered to he seemed to find new life and power. This time however there was a difference and he was forced to rest. The period from 1935 to 1943 must have been hard for him. Those eight years of quiet and relative inactivity must have been a trial, but he never complained. He had known the power of Christ's resurrection, now he would prove the Lord's presence in the fellowship of his suffering.

His wife died in January, 1941 and his daughter May looked after him. His last sermon, on Wednesday, October 27th, 1943, was preached in the Elim Church, Pontardulais where William Llewellyn Bell (who had been pianist at the meetings in Barking in 1925) lived. At the time Stephen was listed as a minister in the Bible Pattern Church Fellowship, a group created by his brother George in November 1940. Stephen played no part in that controversy. He was sometimes unguarded in the things that he said, but he was devoid of guile. It was a fitting tribute that this, his last service should have been in an Elim Church where an Assemblies of God minister was due to hold a crusade. The missioner, Tom Wilson, was one of the converts of the Bishop Auckland meetings in 1927.

Stephen went from Pontardulais to his daughter's bungalow in Porthcawl and it was there on November 17th, 1943, that he died. It was thirty-nine years to the day when he sat under conviction in Siloh Chapel. Stephen's ministry in Elim was of brief duration. His stay with the Assemblies of God was not much longer, but as Alfred Missen, a former General Secretary of the Assemblies of God had said:

'It is not too much to say that his campaigns altered the whole character of the Movement.'

11: Years of Expansion

George's Plymouth meetings in January 1926 began in a small way but in a short time they had so increased that he wrote to E. J. Phillips, who replied on January 19th:

> I am delighted to hear of the glorious times you are having. I intended suggesting yesterday that you should stay longer at Plymouth. You always leave your campaigns when the tide is rising, and I am afraid you are doing the same in Plymouth. If you stayed on and postponed Guernsey and Liverpool, it would be best for Plymouth.

A few days later George sent an overnight telegram:

> 'REVIVAL HERE IF I CONTINUE CAN LIVERPOOL BE POSTPONED REPLY IMMEDIATELY
> PASTOR.'

Phillips telegraphed a fourteen word reply which cost one shilling and sixpence.

> 'GO AHEAD PLYMOUTH AM TRYING TO POSTPONE LIVERPOOL BOOKING
> PHILLIPS.'

Three days later George reported:

> 'I am having the time of my life. Souls are continually flocking to Christ most startling and marvellous healings,

while yesterday hundreds were turned away from the Town Hall an hour before starting time.'

He preached on the near return of Christ. Many of those who claimed to have been healed were asked to give their testimonies and scores did so. He wanted to take a photograph of them all but there was a ban on the use of flashlights owing to the risk of damaging the costly stained glass windows. The few meetings that were held in Devonport Town Hall were packed out as there was only room for 600. There were fifty-five converts in the first three meetings. They heard that they might be able to hire the Military Drill Hall in Plymouth. This was a huge, barn-like structure that could accommodate 6,000. At first, George was a bit cautious about taking this as there was no heating available and it had a concrete floor. At the end of January he wrote to say that the Devonport Town Hall was crowded:

'An average of about forty souls a day are being saved. Three cripples walked in the service last night. The Ambulance brought one and arrangements had been made for it to come for her. However she walked home. This is the greatest healing service yet.'

The success of the Plymouth meetings and the timing of their success caused George Jeffreys to turn his attention in the direction that brought about a consolidation of the Elim work. At the same time it also focused the attention of the public on George himself. This was something that was contrary to his somewhat shy and retiring nature. He had to learn that personal humility and a public image are not necessarily incompatible. He never sought public aclaim for himself, but after Plymouth the name of George Jeffreys was to become associated in the public mind with Elim.

To some, it may seem to be contrary to the words of Paul, who, writing to the Corinthians strongly objected to the claims of those who said, 'I belong to Paul . . . Apollos . . .

Cephas'. George Jeffreys never sought hero worship, but he was conscious of the value of good publicity and was prepared to use it to good effect in the furtherance of the kingdom of God. This is brought out very clearly in one of his letteres to E. J. Phillips. The Elim Publishing Company (established in Clapham 1924) had printed some letters for George as a follow-up for the Plymouth converts. George's original request had specified that the heading should read:

> 'Revival and Divine Healing Campaigns
> Conducted by
> Pastor George Jeffreys.'

The printed form was changed to read:

> 'ELIM REVIVAL AND HEALING CAMPAIGNS.'

He states his reason for choosing the original wording:

> 'The reason why I desire this . . . is because there is scarcely anything (in the eyes of the public) that links me with Elim except as an ordinary worker and any work run on these lines will not succeed. It was alright when Stephen worked with us, but now that he is in opposition I must do something to keep my name before the public. In fact self preservation demands it at present. To this day some people in Plymouth believe that Stephen is the head of Elim and it is difficult to persuade them otherwise.
> It is the chief aim of every successful work to keep before the public the leader of the work. ELIM Revival Campaigns (unless there is some addition) means nothing to strangers, and the first worker that comes along to a district is looked upon as leader of Elim and do what you will it is difficult to persuade them otherwise. We must adopt some proper way of letting the public know. I can see clearly that God intends a work to be built around a channel he chooses and once we loose sight of this, or

take it plain to the public the work suffers. In the near future we will have to contend with the fact that works will arise that will be built around one man's name. If I do not take steps now to preserve my own work the work will suffer.'

Thus, coincidental with Stephen's separation and the delay in the formation of a wider fellowship of churches under the name of Foursquare Gospel Churches of the British Isles Incorporated, George began to develop his own organisation. From now on he would not only gather sheep, he sought to build up a structure in which to pen them.

One significant step was the establishment and subsequent development of the Elim Bible College at Clapham. At the beginning of 1925, sister Hetty Denison suggested that they should start their own Bible School. It was decided that the students should be accommodated in a private house in Clapham and that they should be attached to the Clapham church where Robert Mercer was the minister. Mercer was to be their first teacher. The first students were enrolled in May and the first term ended in November. The first students were Francis E. H. Trevor, later to be a distinguished chaplain in the Royal Air Force, and Jesse Lees, who subsequently became a Church of England vicar. Two others who joined them were James E. Mullen, later of South Africa, and George Thomas from Dowlais. He spent a few years in Mexico and in Spain until the Civil War forced his return. He became secretary to the Elim Missionary Society and served in that capacity for fifteen years. The first classes were held in the minor hall of the Clapham church. At the end of November 1925 the former Redemptorist Convent in Clarence Road was purchased for £6,325. This was known as Woodlands (it stood in four acres of trees), though it was only a few minutes from Clapham Common Underground Station. It remained as the training college of the Elim Church from January 1926 until it was transferred to Capel, Surrey in 1965, following the compulsary purchase order placed on the property by Wandsworth Borough Council who put a high rise housing block on the site.

From Plymouth, George went to Guernsey, where St. George's Hall was crowded with 1,800 to 2,000 people. Some conversions were reported and more than twenty testified to healing in a single service. The Elim work was built upon the foundation of the Vazon Mission that had grown out of George's first visit in 1922. As a result of his second visit the work there was strengthened. There are now four Elim Churches on the Island and it has the largest concentration of Elim members of any place in the United Kingdom.

The postponed meetings in Liverpool eventually started on March 14th. There were a number of Pentecostal meetings in the city, some of them going back to the beginning of the Pentecostal testimony in 1908. None of these meetings were of any size. When George went there he would not link his meeting with any of these groups. He described some of these people as, 'Wild men from Borneo'.

George was very clear in his own mind. He knew exactly what he was attempting to do. Way back in February 1913, when George and Stephen were holding meetings in Penybont, they had told Alexander Boddy that they believed there was a great need for evangelists in the Pentecostal work.

'The Lord is giving the answer through this Revival to the criticism that the Pentecostal people are not interested in Evangelistic work, and only seek to have good times.' During the visit to Liverpool George hired the Boxing Stadium in Lime Street. The headlines of the paper announced:

'Jeffreys In Ring Again.'

Other events outside his control were going to bring his name even more dramatically before the public before the end of the year.

The highly successful meetings in Surrey Tabernacle were continued, and the building was used as the venue for a Convention in Easter 1926. These meetings were to begin on Good Friday, April 2nd. Suddenly, a call was received from the American Evangelist, Aimee Semple McPherson who telephoned from France to say that she wanted to hold meetings in London on her way to Palestine from the United States. This caused considerable consternation at the Elim Headquarters in Clapham. As Aimee was coming to London it was decided that she be asked to take part in the Convention in Surrey Tabernacle. The interest of the press was aroused when they learned of her proposed visit. She had first phoned Clapham on Saturday afternoon, February 27th. She said that she would be in London on the following Thursday, March 4th. They had to rush through publicity material for this short campaign which lasted from Thursday until Sunday. Aimee then continued on her journey to the Holy Land: but she would be back again at Easter.

By any reckoning, Aimee McPherson was a flamboyant character, Born in October 1890, she was converted through the ministry of Pentecostal evangelist Robert Semple. They were married and together they went to China as missionaries where Robert died. The widowed Aimee returned to America with her baby daughter Roberta and set out as an itinerant evangelist. After a few years of hard struggle, she arrived in Los Angeles. She made such an impact there that in 1923 she was able to open the 5,000 seater Angelus Temple. George Jeffreys and his party had visited the Temple during their American tour in 1924 and they had been introduced to Aimee. Aimee Semple McPherson had called her churches 'Foursquare', though there never was any official connection between the American group and the Elim work.

The shortness of Aimee's visit meant that she made very little impact. On her return, the Elim leaders decided that she should be invited to share in their meetings to be held in the Surrey Tabernacle at Easter. Elim had filled the

Top left: George Jeffreys meets Aimee McPherson, 1926.

Top right: The Revival Party: All Foursquare! Principal George Jeffreys, R. E. Darragh, James McWhirter and A. W. Edsor, 1929.

Bottom: George Jeffreys, 1928.

Top: Crowds at Bingley Hall, Birmingham, 1930. *Top left inset:* A few of the thousand baptismal candidates. *Top right inset:* The queue outside.

Bottom left: Stephen and William Jeffreys.

Bottom right: Siloh Chapel, where George and Stephen were converted in 1904.

Top left: George Jeffreys and Lewi Pethrus.

Top right: George Jeffreys' birthplace: No 24 Metcalf Street, Nantyffyllon, Maesteg (in far right of picture). He was born there on 28th February 1889.

Bottom: World Conference crowd, Stockholm, Sweden, June 1939.

Top: George and Stephen Jeffreys enjoying an afternoon's boating, 1924.

Bottom left: George Jeffreys, presiding over a remarkable baptismal ceremony, held at the Albert Hall on Good Friday 1928. Nine hundred members of the Elim Foursquare Gospel Alliance were baptised.

Bottom right: Elim leaders, 1928.

Tabernacle in 1925 without Aimee and it was obvious that with her return the place would not be large enough to cope with the expected crowds. They tried to book several large halls, including Kingsway Hall and Westminster Central Hall, but without success. At that time it was possible to book the Ryal Albert Hall at short notice. There had been conplaints in the press that it was very expensive, consequently it was not as fully booked as it is today. On this occasion it cost £267. 15s, which was a very large sum (in the following year the rent was halved).

Aimee preached on Easter Sunday night (April 4th) and on Monday. The press were there in force and they gave extensive coverage to the meetings. In their coverage of the first visit one of the papers had said that it was a whirlwind revival (there was a very strong gale blowing at the time. Even the much travelled Aimee said the plane ride from Paris was the worst she had ever experienced). Aimee preached a message of some 15,000 words in less than an hour. She presented a striking figure, dressed in white, with a flowing black cape draped from her shoulders, words simply poured from her lips. Yet for all that, the great city was hardly moved. England was not America; the Royal Albert Hall was a far different place from Angelus Temple, even though their outside appearance was similar. A few years later Aimee wrote to congratulate George Jeffreys and to express her delight on hearing the news that the Elim Alliance had bought the Albert Hall (which they had not). After a brief stay in Belfast, Aimee returned to the United States.

On Thursday, May 20th, 1926 her mother sent a cablegram to George Jeffreys:

'SISTER MCPHERSON DROWNED WHILE SWIMMING TUESDAY SOUL GLORIFIED SISTER HAD ANNOUNCED YOUR CAMPAIGN WHOLE WORLD LOOKING TO ANGELUS TEMPLE FOURSQUARE EVANGELIST IMPERATIVE NEED YOU HERE IMMEDIATELY

THIS CRISIS HOUR CABLE EARLIEST POSSIBLE DATE YOU CAN LEAVE
MOTHER KENNEDY.'

George cabled that it was impossible for him to go at the present time, but, in the June 15th issue of the *Elim Evangel* readers were told that:

> 'The Great Angelus Temple Los Angeles (with the largest church membership in the world) which is calling for Pastor George Jeffreys. Will our readers pray that the will of the Lord may be done?'

The cause of all this activity was the disappearance of Aimee. The possibility of going to Los Angeles and of taking over the Temple would occupy the mind of George Jeffreys more than once during the next few years. Involvement with Aimee was to have repercussions that were not always beneficial. Some of his closest associates, especially William Henderson, urged caution. For a new religious movement, almost any publicity had a value, but some of the more flamboyant activities of Aimee did not help George Jeffreys. Her brand of Pentecostalism had to be seen, in the words of Donald Gee, '. . . against her own proper background of the city she made her home – the city of Hollywood and the dramatic'.

Gee went on to say that in his opinion her second visit (really her third in 1928) 'more than the first revealed that she could never have the same magnetic appeal to the more conservative British temperament'.

Aimee turned up again on June 23rd claiming that she had been kidnapped! At this time George was in Belfast. He wired Mrs Kennedy to get confirmation that her daughter was alive.

After the meetings in Belfast George went to Bournemouth for one of his longest Crusades. He began there on July 25th and meetings continued into October. They began at Moordown where Pastor E.C. Blackman had a small Pentecostal Mission. During the first week in the large Canvas Tabernacle 100 people professed conversion. After five weeks the number had increased to 600. For the final two weeks they moved to Boscombe, where people came in such numbers that the Drill Hall in Holdenhurst Road had to be used to cope with the crowds. One of the features of these meetings was the unusually large numbers of men. Mr Blackman was competent enough, but it was obvious that he could not cope with such large numbers: he would need help.

At the conclusion of the meetings they were able to open four assemblies in the area. These were at Winton, Springbourne, Parkstone and West Howe. George sent along Fergus Trevor as the first minister. Trevor had helped to consolidate the work in Plymouth and later was to do the same in Southampton. George was not going to make the same mistake in Bournemouth that he made in Liverpool. In Liverpool he had sent a lady worker as the first pastor and there was a good deal of resentment from some of the men. In Liverpool a different sort of leadership was needed that the lady was unable to supply. There were a lot of men in the Bournemouth meetings, including a number who had been associated with William Oliver Hutchinson's work. Fergus Trevor did not stay very long (it was usual to leave the ministers for only one year at a time). When he was moved 500 people signed a petition which they sent on to Clapham asking for him to be permitted to stay: it had no effect. Trevor himself told the men at Clapham that they should ignore the petition, he said that his successor, J.J. Morgan was doing a good job but that it was to be expected that the people should want him to stay as they always thought very highly of their first minister.

12: Conquest of the North

The call to the north came from the city of Carlisle. Again, as in other places there was a small group of Pentecostals who had been holding out there for almost twenty years. They were regarded with suspicion by other Christians in the district and their conduct gave some cause for concern. On this occasion, owing to the distance, George left the booking of the hall to the local men. They had no idea of what was required. George described the place as an underground cellar without windows and with no ventilation, with a roof that nearly touched his head. The seats were hard, with many having no backs. 'It is', he declared, 'the most awful place I have ever preached in, worse than Hunter Street.'

A hundred people ventured down to the Lower Queens Hall, it was not a promising start. After a few days there were twenty conversions amongst the 200 who were present. On the first Friday there were another thirty-five converted. The tide continued to rise and George had to hastily change his plans. He had announced that he was returning to Ilford on November 21st, but it was obvious that he could not leave Carlisle at this time. He wrote to E. J. Phillips on November 11th:

> 'I do not know what to do about coming from here. The place is literally moved and the whole town is astir. In fact I can see that Carlisle will probably eclipse Bournemouth. There are hundreds of young people captivated the like of which I have never witnessed before. The salvation of souls is marvellous in every meeting, I cannot keep count. The captivation of

> Christians is more marvellous. The cream of the city is now clamouring to get in. The hall we got is a splendid one (seating 500) but about a fourth too small. We are now booking the Drill (Hall) for every possible night. The healings are more and greater than anywhere. Today the place was stirred by a young lad whose arm was in splints and broken. After he was prayed for, his mother took off the splints and the arm was perfect. I cannot possibly tell you how we have gripped the city.'

Not everyone was so thrilled. There was some opposition, especially from the Railway Mission, whose pastor was a Keswick stalwart. He condemned them publicly. One of the reasons for his opposition was that he lost almost all of his young people. One of them, James T. Bradley entered the Elim ministry in the following year. He subsequently spent more than forty-five years in the ministry. He was Dean of the Elim Bible College and Editor for a time. A member of the Executive Council for thirty-four years, he ended his active ministry as Secretary-General.

In Carlisle, as in Plymouth and Bournemouth, they had to hire the largest halls that were available. This proved to be the Military Riding School. The place was like a huge barn, without any form of heating or regular seating. The people were asked to bring their own seats. They came and filled the huge hall, which seated them as close together as possible. They were all clothed in heavy overcoats as a protection against the cold. Once again a strong church was established.

James Walsh, the man who had given the original invitation to George Jeffreys to conduct the Crusade, died in Carlisle on February 19th, 1927. Two months later the converts moved into their own building on the West Wall, where they were to remain for the next fifty years.

George had conducted four Crusades in 1926. In 1927 he increased his activity to such an extent that he held nine Crusades. It was to be the largest number of Crusades that he held in a single year. He began in Rochester where he did not know a single person when he began. Once again there was an encouraging response. Some came out of curiosity and to see the miracles of healing that were reported to be taking place. The meetings were filled with a mixture of the cautious, who were enlightened and revived, and the curious, who were not usually found in religious meetings. Even some of the critics were impressed and some of those who remained, convinced by what they saw and heard.

On January 23rd he opened in Glasgow at St. Mongo Hall. On the first Saturday 600 people came by train from the new church in Carlisle. On arriving in Glasgow they marched in procession to St. Mongo Hall with George Jeffreys leading in his car that was driven by Fred Bell. The first week was not easy, but the crowd from Carlisle gave them some encouragement. Within a short time they were able to report that 150 had been converted. At the end of the month this had risen to 700. By the time the meetings ended on March 28th the number of converts had risen to to 1500. A notable feature of the meetings was the support and interest that was shown by a number of experienced Christian workers who lived in the area. Some of them were experienced ministers of several years standing.

William George Hathaway had been an 'Apostle' with Hutchinson's Apostolic Faith work in the north of England. He had left them after they had gone haywire on the use of prophetic gifts, which were used even in matters of personal decision-making. After he left that group he established a small group of independent Pentecostal Assemblies near Glasgow and at the time he was living in nearby Kilsyth.

Percy G. Parker, a former Congregational minister from Oldbury near Birmingham, was ministering in Glasgow at the Central Tabernacle, George Street (Dr Chalmer's old Church). In his Bible School work in Glasgow, the committee gave him the title of 'Principal Parker'. He had been in Glasgow for three years and he was using a correspondence course which he had written during a two year period in Lynton, Devon.

Both men were very favourably impressed with George Jeffreys. They both joined Elim and within a short time they were both employed at Elim Headquarters. Parker at the Bible College and Publishing Office, and Hathaway in the office. He was appointed as Divisional Superintendent of the London area when that office was created in June 1929.

On March 20th he returned for his third visit to Leeds. On this occasion he would have his greatest success. Although this mission was only a short one, its success was remarkable. Within two weeks 2,290 had professed conversion. The Leeds church was totally inadequate to accommodate such numbers and it became necessary for them to seek alternative accommodation. It is worth noting that each time that George Jeffreys was in Leeds for a Crusade, in 1913, 1920, and now again in 1927, that the increased numbers made it essential for them to seek larger premises. Once again there were a number of outstanding cases of healing.

James Gregson had been a helpless cripple for five years following a serious accident. Hospital treatment was unable to help him and he had to drag himself around on crutches, his legs all twisted. His wife read an account in the local paper describing how a lady had been healed of blindness. She thought that her husband could be healed if only he could get to the meeting. On Sunday he went to the Coliseum where the meetings were being held. Getting there was a great struggle. By this time it was difficult even for fit people to get into the meeting owing to the size of the crowd. Some of the people who were there had pity on him and they took him in through the rear entrance. Some men carried him into the hall and laid him down in front of the platform. One of the Party asked him, 'Brother, you don't look comfortable; can I make you more comfortable?' James replied, 'I am never comfortable,' for he was never free from pain, day or night.

George laid hands on him and prayed. He was healed instantly. When he came to the meeting he had looked very ill; he was only skin and bone. Within the space of two weeks he had put on thirty-three pounds. He was able to return to work as an iron maker. On Easter Monday, April 18th, he was able to travel to the Royal Albert Hall. He gave his testimony before thousands. Five years later he was able to say that he had not lost a day's work since his healing; he was in perfect health.

The meetings in the Royal Albert Hall that year were extensively reported. The *Morning Post* provided the newsagents with a placard which announced:

'LONDON AUDIENCE MESMERISED'

The *Elim Evangel* also gave widespread coverage and they had to print extra copies. The meetings were arranged by E.J. Phillips. He must have had his hands full, for in addition to his work as Secretary-General, he was Principal of the Bible College and Editor of the *Evangel*. Phillips resigned as Principal in April and was replaced by Percy Corry, another former Preston student. Corry had gone out to India on missionary service under the Pentecostal Missionary Union. He resigned in 1915 and joined the army, working his way through the ranks to become a Captain. After the war he spent some time in Belgium and Holland. He joined Elim at this time and became 'Dean' of the Bible College (two Principals were enough). George Jeffreys took the title 'Principal' at this time. The title caught on (in spite of Robert Mercer's protests). Before long E.J. Phillips began to address him as Principal in their letters; after a time this was shortened to, 'Prince'. George addressed E.J. as 'Cardinal' (a reference to the time when he was the pastor of the Armagh Church).

13: Miracles in the South

Following his success at Leeds, George went to Southampton where he held meetings in the new Central Hall on April 21st. Once again the beginning was very small. There were just four converts on the opening night; at the conclusion of the Crusade they were reaching record crowds with 120 converts on the final night. There were some outstanding cases of healing. One of the most outstanding was the case of Florence Munday. She had been sick with tuberculosis of the knee following a fall. She also had a serious skin complaint of long standing.

When George Jeffreys opened his meetings in Southampton Florence was in London where she was staying with a friend. During the time she was in London she was seen by several doctors, but none held out any hope for a cure. Her condition was so bad that her mother was sent for. Eventually her mother returned to Southampton. It was from there that her sister, Ivy wrote to tell her about George Jeffreys' meetings and the healings that were reported in the local newspaper. Florence returned to Southampton on Tuesday, April 26th. It was a very painful journey. Her mother had to carry her from the train to a taxi. She spent the next five days in bed. On Friday, April 29th her mother went to the meeting, while she sat in the gallery of the Central Hall she was healed of anaemic dyspepsia.

On Wednesday, May 4th they took Florence to the meeting in her invalid carriage. She was taken to the front of the hall together with her friend, Hannah Graham, a Wesleyan deaconess and her sister Ivy. George Jeffreys preached that night on, 'Christian Disappointments'. It was just what she needed: she had only been to church four times in the last fourteen years. During the hymn, 'All hail the power of Jesu's name', she felt the power of God falling upon her. Her sister felt it too, and said, 'Florrie, you are going to walk'.

They called George Jeffreys over to them. When he came, he asked, 'How long have you been lying in this old carriage?' Florence told him, 'Fourteen years. I have not walked for fourteen years. The trouble is my knee, it is a wasting disease'. 'Do you believe that the Lord can heal you?' he asked. 'Yes' Florence replied. George asked her to come to the healing meeting on the following afternoon.

There were many people to be prayed for that afternoon. When George Jeffreys came to Florence, he said, 'Sister, do you still believe that the Lord can heal you?' 'Yes', she said, 'but my leg is in a splint'. 'Never mind the old splint', he said, 'You just believe, and pray with me'. He prayed, 'Oh Lord, turn back the disease, and unlock these joints'. As he said that, the power of God surged through her body, shaking the carriage, and she felt the knee bend in the splints. Turning to her sister Hannah, she said, 'All pain has gone'. 'Can you stand?' sister Hannah asked. 'Yes', Florence replied, 'I can', and with that she stepped out of the carriage. George Jeffreys asked, 'Can you walk?' 'Yes' she replied. With that he took her by the hand and walked her across the front of the hall. She was still in the splint but in no pain at all. It was 4 p.m. and the congregation were ecstatic. After two hours Florence was taken to the deaconess's room while the hall was cleared. Her sister took off the splint and discovered that the previously frail limb above the knee had gained two inches in girth. Florence remained in the hall until the close of the evening meeting when she walked up the stairs to the organ and down the other side. The family insisted that she should go home and they put her back into the carriage for the journey but she walked in through the front door to greet her married sister. She went into her ground floor bedroom where she took off the splint and removed the leg cradle from the bed. She slept all night, the first time in fourteen years.

Next morning she noticed that all trace of the skin disease had gone. Her leg, which had been four and a half inches shorter than the other, had grown four inches and was almost normal size, though her knee was still stiff. The leg returned to its normal length while she was staying at the Bible College in London when she had gone there prior to being baptised in the Royal Albert Hall at Easter, 1928. She was one of 1,000 candidates. For thirty years, between 1939 and 1968, Florence Munday pastored the Elim Church in Gosport. She did not retire until she was well into her seventies.

One of the outstanding features of these meetings was the number who were healed, who went on to live long and active lives of useful Christian service.

A good church was established in Southampton, though they experienced considerable difficulties owing to their inability to find suitable premises for a permanent place of their own. They had to use several different places for their meetings; some of these were as much as three miles apart. Eventually, in May, 1929 they were able to purchase a former Wesleyan Church for just less than £3,000 (the original building was destroyed in an air raid in the war).

From Southampton George moved along the coast to Brighton where he campaigned for ten weeks and both Brighton and Hove were stirred. Mrs Coffin, the wife of a local Baptist minister was cured of cancer. An old historic meetingplace, the Glyn Vivian Mission, in the Lanes, Brighton was acquired and this became home to the new Elim congregation.

George went on to Worthing for a few meetings (he returned there for a longer visit two years later). After that he took his tent to Hastings, where, with the increasing interest, they transferred to the Elite Cinema, St. Leonards.

In September he moved to Portsmouth. In fact he transferred to Portsmouth Guildhall and the Coliseum Theatre from Southsea, where his tent on the common soon became too small. There were about 900 converts during the four weeks of the Crusade, which ended on October 2nd. There were also many who were healed. One of these was Christine Jardine. She had been in a bath chair and had been suffering from internal paralysis following a fright twenty years before. She had undergone three operations and had been told that she would never work again. To add to her problems she was also suffering from sleeping sickness (encephalitis lethargica) and was blind in one eye. After prayer and the laying on of hands on Thursday, September 22nd, she was instantly healed. Forty-two years later, a sprightly old lady and still full of life, she signed her name beneath a photograph that was published shortly after she was healed.

The picture showed, 'crippled' and 'Healed'. She wrote:

> 'Before & After. Healed by the power of God. To God be the glory.
>
> 1927-1969 Chrissie Jardine'

As the year drew to a close a series of meetings were held in North London and in Wimbledon. The response was encouraging: there were 500 converts recorded in Hammersmith and a further 1500 at the Alexandra Palace. The results were of greater benefit to the local denominations than to Elim. The Vicar of St Saviour's, Crouch Hill, not only supported the meetings, but wrote about them in glowing terms.

In seeking to record the ministry of George Jeffreys during these years there is little at first to distinguish between one year and another. National and international events come and go, almost without mention in the Elim publications. The only reference to the National Strike is an expression of regret that some of the readers of the *Elim Evangel* who were living outside London had not received copies of the magazine on time.

A description of George Jeffreys the evangelist given by a reporter present at the opening of the Bournemouth church at the end of September 1927 is worth recording:

'Principal Jeffreys is a wonderful evangelist. He has a full round voice that is never used for raving, and large dark eyes that beget confidence. When he speaks others must listen, and when he appeals, he does not appeal in vain. "Pray", he says, or "sing", and his followers would do it. His hold on them is sure; they hang on his every word, and believing implicitly, obey.

It is the quiet, convincing tone in which he speaks that gives Principal Jeffreys much of his evangelical influence. Men sometimes speak of a powerful preacher as one who talks loudly and storms and gesticulates. There is nothing of that about this man. He never shouts, yet there is a fervour and force in the very smoothness of his voice. Sometimes, to give emphasis, he bites off his words at the end. Sometimes he leans slightly forward, urging gently, but passionately, persistently, "If you want to be saved, why not be saved now?" He is not shouting at you, but talking persuasively, as a dear friend.

Very rarely he smiles, and the fleeting gleam that passes over his face seems to leave his dark eyes more serious, more intensely earnest than before. And even more rare than his smile is the swift, dramatic gesture of the outstretched arm and pointing forefinger. He used it once yesterday, and with it came the assurance, soft but vividly startling, "And you shall be saved". His evangelical power is such that faith springs to meet it.'

In 1928, George's activity continued even if it was on a slightly reduced scale. Places visited for longer or shorter periods ranged from Croydon, Reading and Eastbourne to Bath, Exeter and Bradford. Numerically, Croydon was the most successful with 1,600 converts. This was followed by Bradford with 1,400. There could be no greater contrast than that between Eastbourne, with its quiet gentility and its retired admirals and generals, and the wool capital of Bradford. George found a ready response in both places.

The meetings in the Royal Albert Hall in 1928 were

memorable for the huge baptismal service that was held on Good Friday. A special baptismal tank weighing a ton and measuring twelve feet by six feet had to be contructed. It needed a special crew to manhandle it into place in the Hall. When the press reported that a thousand people were to be immersed in the tank during a single service, a prominent physician sought to prevent the service in the interest of hygiene. E.J. Phillips found a simple solution. He had water running in at the one side and out of the other so that it could not be classed as static. There was so much water about that they were in more danger from the electric wires in the area below the tank. The publicity helped to swell the numbers who came to the meetings that year. George Jeffreys could easily fill the Albert Hall without Aimee McPherson (all told he preached there forty-nine times between 1926 and 1939).

When Aimee returned to Britain for a Campaign in 1928, George found that the close association between his own movement and Aimee in the public mind did not help him. In fact it proved a disadvantage, particularly in the Exeter meetings.

During 1928 George gave a good deal of thought to revising the Rules and Regulations by which the Elim Movement was governed. By that time there were more than seventy Elim churches. Another 100 were to be added in the next six years. The basic and simple Rules which had governed the old Elim Evangelistic Band from 1922, were revised several times. These were replaced by new Rules which came into operation early in 1929. There were at least seven separate books of rules. Every one was marked 'Private and Confidential'. There were three forms of government for Elim churches: central government from Clapham; personal government by a minister; local government under deacons. The main body of churches belonged to the first group, which were in the body known as the Elim Foursquare Gospel Alliance. In April 1929 the work was divided into a number of Districts, each with its own Superintendent. Ministers were under strict supervision and were moved every year, usually at very short notice. Many of the ministers were single. Quite a number of these young men left the college after a very short time and some of them were put in charge of churches of up to 800 people. They had to preach about five times a week and do a great deal of visiting. The most that any of them could expect as a mode of transport was a bicycle, costing about thirty shillings (£1.50). At first all the ministers were paid directly from the offerings but later, all the offerings were banked and they were paid from headquarters instead. It was necessary to declare all private gifts in money or in kind. These went into an 'All things Common Fund' and their value was shared between all the ministers: it was a hand to mouth existence at times. Reports had to be sent to the Divisional Superintendent every week and they had to give permission for a minister to be away from his assembly even for a single meeting. It really was like the Salvation Army (without the uniform or the band), the ministers were all pastors or evangelists (a name that was confined to young ministers in their probationary period and to some members of the Revival Party who were not in charge of a church) and George Jeffreys was the general. When he was leading his troops into battle there was none better, they would have followed him anywhere. As an armchair general he would have many problems but that was a few years away. The next few years were to see even greater activity. As far as Britain was concerned George had another six years before he reached the zenith of his success.

14: Increasing Momentum

The outstanding feature of George's activity in 1929 was its extent. From Worthing on the south coast and Ipswich in the east, to Greenock in Scotland and at Cardiff and Swansea, his meetings drew large crowds.

On Sunday, April 7th he held meetings in Greenock, Scotland. There were only a handful present for the first meeting in the Town Hall. Within a short time the news had spread and numbers so increased that the building could not provide enough room for everyone. Hundreds were converted. The local papers gave wide publicity to the meetings. The Editor of the *Greenock Telegraph* as well as the ex-Provost, spoke in glowing terms of the meeting. Whole families were converted. A large Parish Church in the East End of the town was hired on the nights when the Town Hall was not available. Just over a year later this became redundant and it was bought by the Elim congregation. It was to be their home for more than fifty years. In that time the church was to provide the ranks of Elim with more than a dozen ministers, two of whom became President. They also gave the town several members of the local council, including the present Provost, Sir Simpson Stevenson.

From Scotland the Revival Party returned to London. They pitched a tent in Brixton in May and stayed three weeks. There were about 600 converts. 200 were baptised in water in a tank in the grounds of the Elim Bible College. Several papers gave wide coverage to the event. *The Graphic* managed to fill a page with six pictures. One of the papers noted the number of cars that were drawn up outside, but went on to observe that most of the congregation were working class.

At the end of June George returned to the south coast, first to Hove for five days, and then to Worthing where he pitched his 'Canvas Cathedral'. During the time that he was there his mother died at her home in Maesteg. She was seventy-eight. She had lived to see two of her sons achieve a measure of success, but for George, greater success was to follow within a short time. Some of this success was to be in Wales, which, apart from Dowlais had seen very little of him since his first mission with his brother in 1913.

After a brief period in Ipswich in September, he moved to the Cory Hall, Cardiff, starting this campaign on Sunday afternoon, 22nd September. In a letter to E. J. Phillips on the next day he said:

> 'I opened fire on a handful of people here yesterday. I didn't turn them out. Like every other campaign it will take time.'

Three days later he gave a few more details:

> 'We had a few at the meeting on Sunday afternoon, more in the evening and still more last evening. Three decided last night. Good class of people are coming, and there is a real revival atmosphere.'

After three weeks they counted 500 converts. In fifty-one days he preached seventy times. In that period they recorded 1,600 converts. They went from one hall to another as the meetings gathered momentum. From the Cory Hall they moved to Splott Road Baptist Church, and finally they had to use the largest church in Wales, Wood Street Congregational Church, in the centre of the city. Even that was inadequate to provide seating for all who sought admission. This was his most successful crusade to date. The new assembly continued in the Cory Hall. This was hired for a few years at considerable expense. The drain on the finances of the congregation was considerable. It was four years before a piece of ground became available and they were able to lay the foundation for the City Temple. This was opened on March 24th, 1934. It remained the largest Elim Church in Wales as well as being the largest in Britain for many years.

Following his success in the Principality, George went in appalling weather to Swansea. He had hardly been back there since he had gone to the Saturday night meetings in Belle Vue, not long after his first introduction to Pentecostalism in 1910. Beginning in the Central Hall on 11th November, he continued for a month. Once more crowds filled the hall, but he was largely unknown in the town. There was a good deal of confusion, even amongst those who said they knew him; some thought that they were coming to hear Stephen or even his brother William, who had held meetings in nearby Morriston.

On the opening night there were about a hundred present (this was a better start than in most places). Interestingly, the reporter who covered the meetings was the same reporter from the *Daily Express* who had reported on Evan Roberts's meetings twenty-five years before. He compared George with Evan Roberts. George admitted that he had been told before that he was like Evan Roberts.

At the end of the first week numbers had risen to 1,000 and on the second Sunday there was an outstanding case of healing. Glyn Thomas, a twenty-one year old married man was a newspaper seller who had a pitch near the railway station. He had a huge hump on his back and he also suffered from a rupture: he was well known in the town. After prayer and the laying on of hands he was instantly healed. The jacket that he was wearing hung limply on his back and the huge hump had disappeared. He went to the local newspaper office to report his healing and they acknowledged that they knew him and that he seemed to be cured. The report in the *Cumbria Daily Leader*, of 19th November, 1929, was confirmed to me forty years later when some friends were staying in my home. I had lodged with Mr and Mrs Pearce in Cardiff when I was assistant minister at the City Temple in 1953. Jimmy Pearce was reading one of my books (Robert Davragh's, *In Defence of His Word*, 1932) when he exclaimed in excitement, 'Glyn Thomas, from Swansea, I knew him. I used to lodge in his home when I lived in Swansea. At that time he had the hump on his back. I left there and came to live in Cardiff. I never knew that he had been healed'. When we compared the dates, it turned out that Jimmy was living there before the healing took place. He had not joined the Cardiff church until some time later. Glyn Thomas became a minister with the Church of the Nazerene. He died in 1982.

A number of the churches in Swansea sent George invitations to preach for them. Doors were opened everywhere. Kezia would have been even more proud of her favourite son if only she had lived a few months longer.

A few miles away, his old minister, Glasnant Jones was still preaching. One night he came to hear George. What he heard must have brought great joy to the old warrior. The year was one of triumph but there were a few clouds on the distant horizon.

Writing from Ireland in July, after the new Regulations had come into operation, George expressed himself as, '. . . not satisfied yet . . . our working arrangements are the best'. He thought that they were only, 'the means in our hands . . . Until some kind of Presbyterian Government for ministers and Assemblies is decided upon we can expect to see a lot of loose assemblies and workers'. He was worried that some, 'busybodies' who were in touch with the legal position, 'have openly declared that the property belongs to the Church, the people, and not the Alliance'.

During that year also, Edward, Stephen's son was increasingly active. He was working in many areas, often on George's heels, in London and in Wales. When Stephen returned from his world travels he joined his son. There was no malice in Stephen, but it did create friction, especially as the success of Eddie's work developed into the Bethel group of churches. Though it is not proper to consider them as being fully Pentecostal, their emphasis on healing and the huge crowds which they attracted caused confusion in the public mind. George was to be embarrassed more than once as a result of this confusion.

The new year opened with great prospects. Without warning, on 18th January, 1930, an article appeared in *John Bull*. This was a down market *Private Eye*, founded in 1906 by Horatio Bottomley (1860-1933). He had been found guilty on twenty-three counts out of twenty-four of fraudulant conversion and had been sentenced to seven years penal servitude. He was released in 1927. The magazine was often involved in litigation; sometimes they were cleared, often they had to pay damages. The article was entitled, 'Frenzied Victims of Hypnotic Pastors'. It contained a picture of George Jeffreys and his Revival Party. Starting off with a note that the House of Commons were to discuss the accountability of organisations and individuals who collect money from the public, it launched into an attack. It referred to '. . . the money-making methods of a gang of pseudo-religious apostles of faith-healing who for years have obtained immense sums of money from the public, and have never divulged what happens to the revenue'. It went on to name George, Stephen and William Jeffreys as well as Edward. They were linked with others and accused of a number of sharp practices. The article caused consternation in the Elim camp. The accusations were, as far as they were concerned, totally without foundation. In fact George Jeffreys was very careful in all his dealings. His legal adviser and friend John Leech K.C. wanted to make a case of it. In his view the statements were clearly libelous.

George was in Glasgow when the paper came out. He had to face the placards that announced the *John Bull* article. He could not ignore them as they were on sale outside the hall in which he was preaching. The paper was on sale on that Saturday. On Tuesday, in the newly opened City Temple, someone caused a disturbance when they demanded that George should give a public answer to the charges.

George was calm in his reply to the noisy critic. He stated that if anyone thought him guilty they had a remedy. They could take these charges to the Public Prosecutor. The critic and his friends were dumbfounded. The atmosphere in the meeting was electric and the large congregation was very much on George's side.

The Elim leaders took considerable time to frame a reply. E. J. Phillips had been more concerned in his first response that the paper had infringed copyright by using one of George's photographs without permission. Elim's solicitor met the solicitor who acted for *John Bull* but very little came of that meeting. The matter was complicated as several groups were referred to and it was difficult for George Jeffreys to refute the charges that were directed at him without, at the same time implying that they were true of any of the others. Eventually, after several letters had been exchanged between George and E. J. Phillips, George wrote an article, which Phillips revised (after consulting their solicitor). It was entitled. 'A Disclaimer', and it was published in the *Elim Evangel* on February 21st. The tone of the Disclaimer was almost apologetic. It began by declaring:

> 'After much prayerful consideration . . . (we have) decided to confine ourselves for the present to the following reply.'

They went on to say that their reply was not sent forth with any bitter feelings of resentment against the editor of *John Bull.* They denied the charges and declared that they were false.

The language of *John Bull* contained such things as:

> 'A better opportunity has never been provided to put a stop to the moneymaking methods of a gang of pseudo-religious apostles . . .
> . . . their leaders are three brothers, George, Stephen and Willaim Jeffreys . . . they forsook the perils of the pit for the profits of the pulpit.'

The Disclaimer was signed by the Overseers, Divisional Superintendents and departmental heads of the Elim work. They were all men of integrity who lived lives that were beyond reproach. Some of them had made great sacrifice. Those who knew them could testify to their honesty.

The effect of the *John Bull* article was less serious than might have been expected as it had been read by more than a million readers. Many of the Elim converts were shown the article by their workmates. One Elim lady wrote to the editor of *John Bull* in disgust to say that she would never buy another copy of the paper. On the other hand, E. J. Phillips told George Jeffreys that he had heard that a lady who had offered to cover the cost of George's next Campaign withdrew her offer after reading the article.

The *Evangel* article was welcomed by Elim readers and the regular order of 12,000 copies was increased for the one issue. They could not hope to compete with the massive circulation of *John Bull*. Fortunately the matter was dropped in a very short time; most people forgot all about it. *John Bull* had other stories to tell their readers. George Jeffreys continued with his work of evangelism. It was to be his most successful year.

Among many invitations requesting George Jeffreys to hold meetings was one that came from Birmingham. At the end of 1929 it was reported that a large church in Broad Street, Birmingham was up for sale. The minister had emptied the place and the congregation had melted away. As it turned out the building was disposed of very quickly, almost before Elim heard about the matter.

It was in Birmingham in February 1924 that a meeting took place in a small room over a garage in Whitehead Road, Aston. This led to the founding of the Assemblies of God. The success that George had in many towns still left him a little cautious about going to Birmingham. The Elim leaders thought that they should make an initial approach for a church in nearby Smethwick. A building had become available and E. J. Phillips went to see the place. The city was very crowded and he was unable to find a hotel; he spent the night on a seat at the station. The church in Smethwick was acquired for a bargain price of £1,225. They thought that Phil Hulbert should hold meetings there at first. Yet at the very time they were making these plans, Phillips wrote to George Jeffreys concerning a three week mission conducted by Seth Sykes:

> 'It seems to me that all campaigns are practically a failure on new ground, unless they are conducted by you.'

While the Smethwick building was being renovated and they were waiting for Phil Hulbert to come, they learned that the Congregational Church, Steelhouse Lane, in the city was to close. It became available for meetings while its future was being decided.

Birmingham had been a great centre for nonconformity. It had been represented by such diverse traditions as those of the Unitarians and the Congregationalists as well as the Quakers. The Congregationalists had been represented by Dr R. W. Dale and Dr J. H. Jowett; Dale had a great influence on the city. At the other end of the spectrum Cardinal Newman had established the Oratory in the city in 1849 (he died there in 1890). The Anglican Church, whose first Bishop, Charles Gore, had helped to found the diocese in 1905, was represented by Bishop Barnes. He had created a furore in a book entitled, *Should Such a Faith Offend?* He had been a distinguished scientist but denied many of the fundamental Christian doctrines such as the Virgin Birth and the physical resurrection of Christ.

The city was ripe for revival. Both D. L. Moody in 1875 and Dr R. A. Torrey in 1904 had held meetings in the city. They had the advantage of the support of many of the churches but George Jeffreys had no such support. Some 200 churches in the city united in a 'Back to Church' Campaign. This drew together several thousand people who marched in procession, lead by the Salvation Army Band and Bishop Barnes. The effort was not a success.

George Jeffreys began his campaign in Ebenezer

Congregational Church, Steelhouse Lane on Wednesday afternoon March 26th,1930. There were only a handful of people at the first meeting and the following day he reported to E. J. Phillips:

> 'My meetings opened yesterday with a real backwash from the meetings in Dudley (Where Eddie Jeffreys opened on March 16th–such crowds attended his meetings that many were left standing outside). All the people that could not get, or had already received the tickets they had used for healing in Eddie's meeting came to me. It was a real uproar when I invited people out for healing. Although the ground floor of the Church only was full yet they rushed out like wild Indians. Ho (sic) my what a place. In Eddie's meetings he prays with a certain number *one* by *one* on a *chair*. When they found I invited them all out, it came as a surprise. One man said at the end, "This man is a better preacher but the other performs more than he does".
>
> Last night was a better meeting, floor full and some in the gallery. This afternoon a splendid D.H. meeting with an entirely new kind of people eighty-nine conversions this afternoon.'

The next day he was to write:

> 'Fairly good meetings again last night, no healings. I simply preached, forty-three saved. The spectacular methods of Eddie certainly outshine our work.'

Within five days the church was full. The number of converts continued to rise. Something had to be done. Some days there would be large queues waiting for the building to open. After a month they hired the Town Hall for four days. Even this proved to be too small; they announced that they would use the huge skating rink (the Embassy Rink in Walford Road was the largest in Europe). The *Elim Evangel* said: 'Visitors are assured of admittance as there is accommodation for 8,000 people.' The meetings continued for the four Sundays in May, both in the afternoon and at night. The crowds were so large that they had to look for an even bigger place. For the final two weeks they moved to the massive Bingley Hall Exhibition centre, off Broad Street, This was used for shows and trade exhibitions and had a capacity for for some 15,000 people (fire regulations were not so strict in those days. Others who have used the hall in later years did not occupy the same area that George used). Even this huge hall was stretched to the limits at times to accommodate the crowds. George preached at twenty-six meetings in Bingley Hall. The number of converts went up from the 600 recorded after five days to more than 10,000. Even that number is probably below the actual response. A distinguished visitor, Rev. R. J. Jones J.P., who was present at a number of meetings counted the converts on more than one night and he recorded a higher figure on each occasion.

The *Birmingham Gazette* asked us to:

> 'Imagine Bingley Hall crammed with seats and every seat occupied. Imagine the galleries crowded and people wedged tight in doors left open to let in the air.'

The Hall had been used by Evangelists on two previous occasions. D. L. Moody and Ira D. Sankey were there during Moody's second visit to Britain in 1875. Dr R. A. Torrey and Charles Alexander had used the building again in 1904. Both visits had the support of a large number of churches. George had no such support.

The Revival Party, consisting of Robert E. Darragh as song leader, Albert W. Edsor as pianist and James McWhirter as organiser, with George Jeffreys as the preacher, took the city by storm. This was their most successful Crusade. The effects of these meetings were felt far and wide, not only in Elim but in the lives of so many. Even now, more than fifty years after it is by no means uncommon to meet those who were converted in those meetings, or whose parents were. In addition to the large number of converts more than a thousand testified to the fact that they had been healed. In three services they baptised a total of 1,000 converts.

One of the converts, Olive Reeve later joined her friend Harriet Fisher in Hockley where they founded the well-known Hockley Mission. They have a multi-racial congregation in a needy area of the city and minister to several hundred. Another convert, Gerald Chamberlain was only a boy at the time; he went on to become an Assemblies of God minister and helped to found the Pentecostal Child Care Association. Within a short time there were three Elim Churches in Birmingham. By 1936 there were eleven.

After only a short break George went for a brief visit to Switzerland. In later years he was to have even more converts there, but this was a short holiday.

In July he returned to London where he conducted a short campaign in Wandsworth. In August he moved on to Kingston on Thames where he spent three weeks. At the end of August and early September he moved to Ealing. London was not so easily moved; perhaps it was too large and its various outlying districts too self-contained.

On September 13th Elim hired the magnificent Crystal Palace for the first time. Built in 1850 by Sir Joseph Paxton for the Great Exhibition of 1851, it was transferred from its Hyde Park site to Sydenham in1853-4. Elim made use of Crystal Palace at various dates each year between 1930 and 1936. The meetings were a great success and drew huge crowds. On a number of occasions they baptised converts in a tank in the Bandstand. They were there for the last time in 1936 when they had their 'Coming of Age Celebrations'; shortly after that the Palace was destroyed by fire. George was holding meetings in Camberwell at the time and he drove over to see the shattered remains.

It was a year of trials and triumphs. Opposition and criticism from the secular press was to be expected (George had a very good press coverage. A press cuttings agency sent copies of all the reports on George's meetings and hardly any were critical. The biggest problems came when they confused George with the names of his brothers or his nephew. The *Daily Mail* produced an awful report claiming 'Three people go mad after "faith meeting" '. They quoted this in their report on George's death in 1962. The story was a distortion of one of Stephen's meetings. George was nowhere near the place. They did apologise when this error was pointed out to them).

The worst, and the most violent attacks came from religious writers. Arthur H. Carter, Editor of an extreme, and short lived periodical the *Bible Witness*, wrote several strongly worded articles which attacked George Jeffreys. A.J. Polock wrote against George Jeffreys in strong terms in his pamphlet, *Modern Pentecostalism, Foursquare Gospel, Healing and Tongues.* These were a few of the trials that George had to endure at that time. He did not stop his evangelistic work and he remained in the London area until the end of October. Two weeks were spent in Kensington. Horbury Chapel, where Stephen had preached in 1921, was acquired and extensively renovated. It was opened on the last day of January 1931 and re-named Kensington Temple. Today it has the largest congregation of any Elim Church in Britain. There is a multi-racial congregation in excess of 1,000 who are served by a team of ministers. At the conclusion of the Kensington meetings George opened a crusade in Nottingham on October 29th. Meetings continued for several weeks and drew large crowds. Once again a famous preaching place of a former generation was acquired. The massive Halifax Place Chapel, former home of the Methodists had a capacity of 1,800. It was built in an Italian style; outside there were Ionic columns and inside the ceiling was ornately decorated. It was said to have the highest ceiling of any Methodist Church. The building was re-named the City Temple.

A well-known Wesleyan local preacher who attended the meetings reported that on the day he was present out of a congregation of at least 1,600: 'As far as I could see, there were not six of them that I knew. The bulk of the congregation seemed to me to be men and women who were connected with no church'. It was an impressive testimonial to the fact that many of Elim's converts were being drawn from the ranks of those who were not regular churchgoers. In later years the Nottingham Church was to be very seriously affected by trouble that resulted in George setting up another organisation. Many of those who were converted in this first visit were to help form the nucleus of a number of new assemblies in the area. The city has since become the location for the offices of the Assemblies of God.

In November, Edward Jeffreys was in the Potteries. He was refused the use of the hall belonging to the local council. This came about after the Medical Officer of Health had declared that Edward had removed splints and a frame from the limbs of a patient who was undergoing treatment. This was widely reported by the national papers, the *Daily Express, Daily Herald* and the *Sketch*. Some of them carried photographs; the picture was of George Jeffreys. All of the papers issued an apology. George wrote to E. J. Phillips:

> 'The photo in the Manchester edition of the *Daily Sketch* is a freak. I hope to goodness they won't say it is my photo, it simply said "Pastor Jeffreys". It is an awful looking thing with a mouth wide open and teeth sticking out half a mile. The forehead was mine although the head was bald. So you need not bother about claiming that as mine.'

There was no truth in the claim that Edward had removed any splints. The council gave their permission for the meetings to continue. Even the highly respectable *Lancet* gave a space to the story.

15: Chronicle Of the Years

The year of 1931 began with George in Belfast. He had spent very little time in Ireland since they had moved the offices from University Avenue, Belfast to London in 1924. The work in Ireland had been considerably neglected; he had been busy building up the work on the mainland.

William Henderson had been one of the Overseers and he was appointed Irish Superintendent in June 1929. He left Ireland and was in charge also of the Southern District in England fron June 1929 to April 1930. Henderson's responsibility for Ireland came to an end in December 1929 and he was replaced by Joseph Smith: Smith lived in London. Ireland did not have its own Superintendent until J.J. Morgan was appointed in May 1933; the office was abolished in May 1934. Tragically, Henderson died of a cerebral haemorrhage on the last day of June, 1931, at the age of fifty-two. He left the residue of his estate to the Alliance. This amounted to £5. 7. 6.; there was not enough to pay for a memorial stone over his grave. His wise advice was to be missed in later years. He was known as 'Henderson the Good'. There was hardly any important decision that George Jeffreys made without first consulting Henderson. It is probable that many of the decisions that were made after his death would have been different if he had lived.

George found that there was a very good response to his ministry in Ireland on this occasion. At Armagh, the local paper went so far as to say that the city had not passed through such a spiritual experience since the days of St. Patrick. At Portadown, they had such an exciting time it was said that the Parliamentary election was tame in comparison. So many sought admission to the Town Hall that there was a danger of serious injury. The Town Clerk personally offered them the use of the new market for meetings and thousands assembled. A notable feature of these meetings was the number of men who attended.

The crowds who came to the meetings in Belfast gave reason for encouragement. Twenty-three converts were recorded on the first afternoon. A further fifty-six were added at night. They sold almost 400 magazines and fifty copies of *Ministry of the Miraculous*, however, they did not establish a new church.

Early in February, George wrote to the Elim Headquarters in Clapham to report that there were, '. . . rows and revivals everywhere'. Many of these troubles had arisen as a result of the introduction of the new Rules in May 1929. The elders who had existed since the early days George had called 'permanent elders'. They were replaced by, 'Church Officers'; these held office as Secretary and Treasurer and after three years they were all to be replaced. This again caused friction, particularly in Ireland. Under the new rules churches had to take up an offering at every meeting. This was particulary hard when most churches had six meetings each week. There were many who were unemployed and a lot of young people.

In the early period many of the Irish churches were served by the senior ministers and most of the ministers were known to the people. With the growth of the work a number of younger ministers from England were introduced. An Irish Superintendent, based in Ireland, would have made things so much easier. The problems that were being experienced in Ireland contained the seeds that would cause a crisis in the Movement within a few years. These issues concerned such matters as lay representation, ownership of property and local control, as distinct from central control from Clapham. George did not introduce any changes at this time; he was still convinced that central government was the best, both from a practical and from a scriptural point of view.

James McWhirter was busy in Lancashire making arrangements for George to hold meetings there. George announced that he was proposing to change his policy. He decided that he would revisit many of the assemblies and seek to build them up. As a result the Bible College was practically closed. A number of men from Ireland went directly into the work without going to college. There was still a severe shortage of suitable young men for the ministry.

To add to the problems, James McWhirter discovered that Edward Jeffreys had booked the same site in Blackpool where George had been going to have meetings. If George had gone ahead with his plans they would have pitched their tents next to each other on St. Anne's Road, Blackpool. George had announced that he was going there and this was published as early as April. When he learned that Edward was going to do the same, George withdrew so as not to cause any problems. The *Bethel Messenger* issued a fierce statement and the *Elim Evangel* published a reply. It was not very edifying. The local paper commented:

> 'The piquant spectacle of uncle and nephew conducting rival revivalist campaigns is to be a feature of the season in Blackpool.'

Phil Hulbert was substituted for George Jeffreys; George returned to Blackpool later in the year and a church was established.

Other places visited at this time were Huddersfield, Knottingley, Barnsley and Sheffield. Churches were established in each place. In Glossop, the work had previously been associated with Beth Rapha Healing Home and Pastor Richard Howton. It was in Glossop that the meeting of the Northern District took place in October 1932. A year later the first Elim Conference was held. During the early part of the Second World War some of the departments of Elim Headquarters were transferred to Glossop for a short time.

In Halifax there had been a Pentecostal work associated with the Emmaus Mission that was run by Joseph Walshaw and his wife Lydia. For many years, in the twenties, Emmaus gave more than a thousand pounds per year to missions. Both Mr and Mrs Walshaw lived to a great age; he to ninety-four and she to ninety-seven. It was a common sight to see him present at meetings before his death in 1945 (with a flowing beard, he could be picked out in the front row at youth meetings). He helped to frame the Model Trust Deed which gave responsibility to local trustees in Elim Churches. It was based upon the Methodist Deed that had originally been drawn up in Sowery Bridge near Halifax.

This year did not draw such large congregations as 1930 but as far as new churches were concerned, the largest number was established apart from the record year of 1927. The seventy churches that had been established by 1928 rose to almost 100 in 1930. By 1933 they totalled 153. By any standard this was a remarkable rate of growth. Many of these churches were very large, particularly by modern standards.

The tent that was pitched on Smithfield Fairground in Sheffield in August was soon covered in grime, but it became the birthplace of some 2,000 souls.

In January 1931 E. J. Phillips wrote to George Jeffreys to tell him that a Congregational minister who was teaching in a seminary in Stockholm had paid him a visit at Clapham. The man was calling upon leading ministers in Britain and he had also visited Dr Orchard, minister of Kings Weigh Church. Orchard told him that in his opinion the future of religion in Britain would be in the hands of the Roman Catholics on the one hand and on the other side with the Fundamentalists, with the 'Foursquare at the head'. E. J. added:

> 'If only Dr Orchard knew the actual rate of progress, and our difficulties therewith, he would have had a different story.'

This was E. J. Phillips at his most pessimistic. Some of the problems were caused by a chronic shortage of money. As the rate of growth and the number of churches increased there were obvious logistical problems from time to time. Anyone who has ever bought a house will know how difficult that can sometimes be. If these sorts of problems are multiplied many times over, then you add the need to move men around the country, often at short notice, it will give some idea of what is involved. In some places it was almost impossible to find a suitable building in which to house the converts. Elaborate plans could not be made beforehand as it could not be known in advance what measure of success would be achieved in any place. It is to be noted that, almost without exception longer campaigns in the larger towns were far more successful than short visits to large or small places. Two examples (out of many) can be cited:

'In Cardiff the meetings in the Autumn of 1929 were very successful. A large group were left after George Jeffreys moved on. They continued to meet in the Cory Hall where the meetings had first been held. The rent of the Hall was a considerable drain on their finances during the next four years. There was a deficit on their accounts during the whole of this time. In 1931 the financial returns were the worst bar one. In 1932 they were worse (though the amount was less) than any other. Things did improve gradually but it was only when they were able to purchase a piece of ground and build a place of their own that there was a real improvement. After that they were always amongst the top churches.

With regard to their numbers, it is worth noting that George Jeffreys was very cautious about making these numbers public, especially with the number who were present at the meetings after he had gone. The Elim Church has kept detailed statistics on all its churches since 1930. When the *Elim Evangel* published the figures for the number who were present at the first communion service in the new Cardiff Church, George said he would have given anything to have prevented these figures being printed. He went on to explain that these figures gave a false picture of the success of a campaign. Writing from Cardiff on November 29th, 1929 he said:

"It is impossible to estimate the numbers who are won until months pass. The first attenders are usually the bolder ones.

In future I should see the reports of these fellows after the Revival Campaigns."

The nature of the financial problems can be illustrated by the experience of the Bradford Church. Following the Campaign they rented the Freemasons Hall in Westgate. They were paying £7 per week in rent and they reported it was difficult to meet the expenses. They asked for a substantial reduction. Following George's second visit they moved into their own building in March 1933 and their financial problems were solved.'

1932 was to be a less active year as far as the number of Crusades were concerned. Churches were established in Dundee and Edinburgh; the first of these was very successful.

There were several unusual events during the year. On February 29th, being leap year, George received a proposal of marriage. In July he had his bible stolen; the thief returned it to him and enclosed a note with her address. Invitations to preach continued to arrive regularly in Clapham. A pressing invitation came for George to hold meetings in South Africa and there were tempting offers from the United States.

The first intimation that America wanted him came in a communication from Los Angeles in June. It was marked 'Confidential'. George wrote immediately to ask E. J. Phillips what he should do. He asked, 'How can I treat it as such from you – we are one'. A few months earlier when there was a possibility that George's brother, Stephen might work with Elim once more, George wrote to Phillips and expressed the opinion that Stephen,

> 'Will never work to the satisfaction of Elim unless you are prepared to give him a real good position such as the headship or even Secretary-General. If the D.S.'s think he would be an asset then I have no objection to Stephen being offered the nominal head of the work. I can easily work behind the scenes, and to tell you the truth will gladly do so, so long as I shall be free to come and go as I feel led. Of course, after your experience with Stephen if you think he could be worked then I simply say, GO AHEAD! I am quite willing but do not encourage such a course because I feel it will be disastrous. Yet I will abide by your decision.'

A telegraphed message arrived from Los Angeles:

> 'ANGELUS TEMPLE INVITES YOU TO TWO OR THREE MONTHS CAMPAIGN DURING SISTER'S ILLNESS CABLE DATE TERMS EXPECT MIGHTY BLESSING CABLE
> HARRIET JORDAN SECRETARY'

George was very much inclined to accept the invitation. He proposed to take some of his Revival Party (Darragh and McWhirter) with him as well as E.J. Phillips. He thought that it might be possible to take over Angelus Temple and for the two works to be linked. When the leading ministers were consulted they urged caution and the idea was dropped.

Instead of going to America in September George went to Edinburgh in October. The *Edinburgh Evening Despatch* described the scene in the Usher Hall.

> 'The air was electric . . . There was a unanimity of enthusiasm for everything that Mr Jeffreys said . . . The

sheer magnetism of the man dominates. He is no roaring tub-thumper. He has a quiet, cultured voice, soft and musical. He speaks in elegant phrases, sometimes speaking above the heads of the people, at other times curiously elementary. All classes are represented. The humble poor, the well-off, the fur-coated and jewelled, the young and aged.'

At the end of the year he was again busy reshaping the working arrangements. He declared that he was, '. . . leaning toward making provision . . . in order that all the churches be the direct property of the Organisation'.

On August 17th, 1933 George was in Hull where he held meetings in a large tent. E.J. Phillips wrote to tell him that Madame Caille from Switzerland wanted to know how old he was. She wanted to know what year he was born. Phillips asked, 'Shall I tell her that we usually keep these things private in this country?' He went on to say that in the August issue of her magazine there was a description of George which began with the words, 'George Jeffreys is forty-four years old'. Phillips added, 'From where she has heard this misinformation, I do not know. What shall I tell the good lady?'

George was forty-four years old, he celebrated his birthday on February 28th at the family home in Neath Road, Maesteg. His youngest sister Chrisley had stayed on in the home, which was named 'Elim', after his mother died in 1929. She stayed there until her death in her ninety-first year in 1985. Another sister, Emily (Mrs Lucas) had her birthday on March 1st. When they were young they had a combined birthday party on February 28th. In 1933 he wrote from the family home:

'I cannot say how long I will be here. I am very much run down and might take some time to get well. In the natural I feel pretty bad with more boils.'

At the time he was revising the manuscript for his book,

Healing Rays. On March 22nd he wrote to say that he was, 'very much cast down with these boils. Can scarcely hold up my head'. E.J. Phillips told him that he should eat nothing but fresh fruit for a week or more and he would find that the boils would disappear. Whether he took this advice or not we do not know. Shortly after this he began an extensive tour of the churches. He covered a large part of the south of England. In some places he stayed for only a single night (Southampton, Worthing, Hove, Rochester and Hastings) other places he stayed two or three days. The places visited included Ryde, Exeter, Plymouth, Yeovil, Portsmouth, Eastbourne and Bournemouth. Each place yielded its crop of converts. The visits were of too short a duration to have any dramatic effect. There were forty converts in Worthing, ninety-five at Hove and 108 in Brighton.

The year had begun with a Crusade in Aberdeen in January and February. There were 400 converts and a church was established. During the rest of the year George consolidated the work in a number of churches. He opened buildings and laid foundation stones in several places. He was in Reading in April, in September he was at Sparkbrook, Birmingham and in March he opened the Southend Hall, seating 875 people. A short Crusade which coincided with the opening had to be extended to cope with the crowds; there were 500 converts.

A short visit to Switzerland resulted in 200 converts. George managed very well and did not feel restricted when he had his messages translated into French and German.

Meetings in Hull were extended to five weeks and 1000 converts were reported. Hundreds were baptised in a portable baptistry in a tent. The meetings were transferred to the City Temple, Hessle Road on September 24th. At the end of September and during October he was in Bangor, Co. Down. In November he had meetings in Scarborough where there were another 400 converts.

Travelling from place to place in their Chrysler, the Revival Party lived in a seventeen foot caravan. They parked on sites, sometimes many miles from the place where the meetings were held. There was only a short respite in a very busy year. In spite of the activity, the number of new churches was the smallest on record.

In addition to his campaign work George devoted a great deal of time to giving further thought to changing the method by which the denomination was governed. In the early days he was in sole control. There had been Overseers for a few years but they never met as a body. When there was any business to be discussed, apart from the long and regular letters that passed between the Principal and his Secretary-General, there was the Annual Meeting of the Elim Evangelistic Band in Belfast over Christmas and New Year. This had virtually come to an end after the move to Clapham. The small group of Divisional Superintendents and the men at Headquarters were consulted from time to time but the rest of the ministers had no say at all. A few ministers were called together at the Bible College in 1929 and they were asked about their ideas prior to the revision of the regulations in May, 1929. Robert Tweed, who was responsible for the Northern District that covered all churches from Birmingham to Dundee, called a Conference in Glossop in October 1932: they met for three days. George Jeffreys was present for part of the time and the meeting was thrown open for suggestions. There was no formal agenda. On September 18th, 1933 the first Ministerial Conference of the Elim Foursquare Gospel Alliance met in London. They met for five days. The Principal told the ministers and their wives that it was necessary to make changes in the government of the Alliance. He asked for suggestions for the future and invited criticism of the present method of government. There were lengthy discussions. They considerd the question of Lay Representation but thought that it was inadvisable at present but that provision should be made for its possible adoption in the future.

Writing from Hull in August, George said that, 'he was working from morning till night trying to get some shape the local church working arrangements, Model, Deed and other things'. Such matters were to take a great deal of his time over the next few years. One scheme after another was proposed, revised, amended and then abandoned. From the beginning Elim had recognised several forms of government. These were: central government from Headquarters; personal government under a minister who had founded a local church; local government under deacons. Most of the larger churches were in the Central Government group (they were known as section A). In 1938 there were eighty-nine in this group and ninety in the other groups. A number of churches had expressed a desire to join Elim and many of them were looking for a larger measure of freedom than that which existed in Central Government. George thought that many of these things could be brought in under the Local Government Scheme. At one time it was thought that as many as twenty-five churches would join. In the end about thirteen joined; in the majority of cases there were more liabilities than assets. Much of George's efforts in the next few years would be devoted to this section but he did not achieve the same success as in previous years. He ended the year with a series of meetings in Ashford, Kent. The meetings ran from December 4th-11th. There was only a limited response and after ten days there were only twenty conversions. Robert Smith, a former member of the Evangelistic Band was the local pastor.

1934 saw the introduction of the Deed Poll on April 10th. The legislative authority was transferred from the Principal and the Secretary-General to an Executive Council of nine. Four of these were elected; three were the Principal's nominees (he had wanted four) the other places were occupied by George Jeffreys and E.J. Phillips. The Council became the supreme governing body until the Deed of Variation of January 14th, 1942. The Council direct the denomination between the Annual Conferences; but the Conference has been the final authority since 1942. It is the duty of the Council to carry out the wishes and directions of the Conference.

The year was also to give George Jeffreys his last major pioneer Crusade in Britain. It was the last large scale campaign that led to the founding of a big church in Britain.

The city of York was the place where the American Evangelist, D. L. Moody and the singer, Ira D. Sankey held their first meetings in Britain in 1872. George Jeffreys had his last major crusade in the city. There were only a tiny handful of Elim supporters in the city before George went there in February. His success was described as being beyond expectation. There were 116 converts by February 8th. When the meetings came to a close on March 11th they had recorded 1,500 converts. The meetings were held in the Exhibition Building, first in a small hall, but before long they needed the large hall. After the Crusade was over they used a large building in the town centre and later, in January, 1937 they purchased the building in Swinegate for £5,000. It was the largest sum that Elim had paid for a building (apart from Kensington Temple, which George Jeffreys paid for). It is interesting to note what George Jeffreys says about his main supporters (and these were the chief ones who invited him there).

> 'My main supporters believe God is fulfilling prophecy in the British Empire.'

He went on to suggest that W. G. Hawkins should be sent as the first minister. He gave as one of the chief reasons for his choice:

> 'He is sympathetic with the Israel question and he will deal with it and there will never be occasion for trouble.'

The subject of British Israelism was raised on a number of occasions in Elim's history. George Jeffreys had accepted this view as early as 1920 (probably through the influence of K.C. and friend, John Leech). The matter was raised at the Northern District Conference in 1932. The Minutes record that:

'This was briefly discussed, when Principal made a proposal that Elim should admit the identity.'

In the following year it was raised at the first full Conference. It was dealt with under the heading 'Supplementary Belief' (matters that were outside the statement of the Fundamentals; for example Partial Rapture, was discussed). On a show of hands sixteen signified that they accepted the identity. It was generally agreed that it should neither be preached nor attacked in the churches.

The subject continued to cause friction, particularly when a few people (not ministers) regarded this as something that should be propagated with an almost missionary zeal. It caused problems in Sheffield and a few of the London churches. The subject was brought up again at the 1934 Conference in September. It was arranged that there should be a debate on the issue and that at the conclusion there should be a vote taken. Percy Corry, Dean of the Bible College and former Captain in the Indian Army was to speak against. The case in favour was to be put by John Leech M.A., Ll.B., K.C.. Leech was a Gold Medalist for Oratory (Legal Debating) and the first honoursman of Trinity College, Dublin. For three years he had been a judge of the Belfast Recorder's Court and of the County Court of Antrim.

At the last moment, Percy Corry backed out. It fell to E. J. Phillips to put the case against the identity. He stayed up all night to prepare. The debate began on the morning of Tuesday, September 18th. Mr Leech put the case for the identity and the Conference discussed this for the rest of the morning. Other business was dealt with during the rest of the day. On Wednesday the Conference returned to the matter and devoted the morning and afternoon to the subject. After Mr Leech had given his reasons why he accepted the identity his address was discussed. E. J. Phillips then gave reasons why he considered the teaching to be false. He was questioned and his address discussed.

One of the questions that was raised was whether the subject should be taught in the churches. The Conference decided:

> '... evidently unanimously that it should be neither preached nor attacked in any Elim Church under Direct Government, nor should any minister under Direct Government appear on any B.I. platform.'

With regard to the rest of the churches, it was agreed by a majority that it should be, '... permissible to preach it within certain limits provided that it would not harm in any way the rest of the work'. A vote was taken and out of seventy-eight ministers who were full members of the Conference, only thirteen accepted the identity. Of the rest, only four out of fifty-three accepted. The printed minutes added:

> 'At the request of the Principal, the result of the voting was not announced at the meeting.'

These minutes were not made available to the members of the Conference. In the following year the matter was raised again:

> 'The Principal suggested that there should be liberty to preach British-Israelism in the Direct Government Churches.'

The subject came up in the evening of the second day of the Conference. It was adjourned until the evening when the Ministerial Session were unable to come to any definite decision:

> 'A serious difference of opinion amongst the members of the Executive Council was disclosed and the meeting broke up without any solution in sight.'

Two days later, on Thursday, October 24th:

> 'The Principal announced that the Executive Council had reached a unanimous decision on the dispute discussed on Tuesday night . . . the Principal promising not to confine his interests to the Local Church Government section, and in particular to arrange a Jubilee Tour in Direct Government Churches. The Principal further promised that he would never bring up the subject of B.I. again at the Conference.'

The Conference declared that

> '. . . it has never imposed any definite ban on teaching B.I. in any Elim Church, its Ministers mutually agree that for the purpose of preserving unity it shall . . . neither . . . propagate it nor attack it in any Direct Government Church. It . . . considers it inadvisable for any minister under Direct Government to appear on any B.I. platform.'

There were those who suggested that some members of the Council or of the Conference had been muzzled. Mr Phillips told the Conference on the following day that he was disturbed by this suggestion and he assured the meeting that no one had been muzzled or coerced in the settlement that had been reached.

A sign of that conflict is seen in the record of the Executive meeting of October 23rd, 1935.

> 'A settlement was reached in the dispute . . . and the teaching of British-Israelism, on the following basis . . . The Principal further promised never to bring up the subject of B.I. again, either in the Executive Council or the Ministerial Conference. Pastor McWhirter assured the Council that he would not preach B.I. in Direct Government Churches and he would avoid such subjects as might lead to his message having a B.I. colouring.'

The Principal would not sign the minutes of the meeting until he had crossed out the words, 'either (in the) Executive Council' and the words in the last sentence, 'and that he would avoid such subjects as might lead to his message having a B.I. colouring'. He initialled the deletions. It is signed, '23rd October 1935 8 p.m.!' When the Conference met on the Friday they recorded that:

> 'The Principal was satisfied because the work could proceed without further debts being incurred and he was satisfied because the subject of B.I. was never to be brought up again. The Council was unanimous, he said in its decision.'

That did not happen. The matter was to be raised again, both in the Council and at the Conference. It formed a substantial part of the Correspondence that passed between the Principal and the Executive Council in the years from the end of December 1936 until well into 1938.

At the time George was living at No. 10 Clarence Road, Clapham and the office in which E. J. Phillips worked was just two doors away. The letters that passed between them started as normal letters covering all aspects of the Elim work. The two men worked in the closest harmony. They did not always agree on everything but the relationship was one of mutual trust, built up over many years. During the series of letters that began at the end of December 1936 and which ran on into 1937, this relationship began to show signs of strain.

It is clear from the reaction of the Conference, and from the tone of the letters, that there was a shift from the consideration of the latest scheme of the Principal, to a fear over what looked like an attempt by him to open the door to allow the introduction of B.I. teaching in Elim. The position was aggravated in 1937 by the publication of a book, *Britain and Palestine in Prophecy*, Methuen. Its author was James McWhirter, who had been one of the Principal's nominees on the Council. The chapter, 'Is Britain Israel?' produced a very strong reaction,

McWhirter, who was head of the young peoples' work in Elim, was clearly in breach of the agreement on this. The 1937 Conferencc reaffirmed the 1935 Resolution and agreed that it should be published in the *Elim Evangel.*

At the same meeting it became clear that there were wider issues at stake. In the evening, W.G. Hathaway, in the absence of E.J. Phillips (he was ill and had to be admitted to a Sanatorium), felt that it was necessary to make a statement to the meeting. All of these conferences were recorded by E.J. Phillip's secretary and stenographer, Mabel Dalton. The later minutes were extracted from these and were circulated to members of the Executive Council who agreed that this was a true record. They were not generally available to members of the Conference. The 1935 minutes take up thirteen pages; those of 1937 occupy nineteen.

After reading the resolution, Hathaway referred to the persistent rumours that had been going around that the Principal was leaving Elim and starting another movement. He went on to explain that the Principal was anxious to clear up one or two difficulties and make some adjustments; then he would be satisfied to leave the Executive to carry on the work and to co-operate with them in every possible way. On the following day the Principal suggested that there should be two sections of the Movement. A Jubilee Concentration with its own Executive and a Forward Movement. The Conference reached no firm conclusions on this matter, but that such rumours should persist was disconcerting, and it was small wonder that one minister (John Dyke, who subsequently became a member of the Executive) should feel it necessary to say that, 'the tide has gone out' for Elim.

When George Jeffreys finally left Elim, British Israelism was not the reason, but it was a contributory factor. It also helped to cloud the issues which resulted in suspicion on both sides. The outcome of these issues was yet to be seen; the effects were noticeable not only in the tension and the anxiety that was caused, but as far as the evangelistic work of George Jeffreys was concerned, there was a slackening of the pace as well as a lessening in the measure of success. At the time these things did not appear to be directly linked.

A number of other factors also played their part in bringing George to a conviction that he must change his methods. The first factor was the success of his visit to Switzerland in June, 1934. At the same time when he was finding less response in Britain he had 6,000 converts in less than a month. Each town that he visited yielded a fresh crop; there were 500 in Zurich, 700 in Berne, and in Geneva there were 1,800 converts recorded in three days. The congregation on the closing night represented twenty-nine nations. Dr Emil Lanz, President of the Swiss Revival League testified that he had established the Revival League in Berne four years before and this was a direct result of George's Birmingham Campaign.

The second factor was the state of George's health. He had carried out a very busy programme for twenty years with hardly any let up. In July 1927, Alexander Boddy, then living in retirement, wrote to George:

> 'I often wonder how you can keep on at such high pressure. May our loving God stand by you for ever. Evan Roberts, Dr Dowie and others who were mightily used, went under through the greatness of the strain, but he can keep you . . .'

George had no outside interests. His only relaxation was being driven by car from place to place.

On December 9th, Stephen collapsed at Becontree. Only a few days before, George had written to Dr Adams of Nantwich, Cheshire when he had asked for an explanation of the disagreement between the brothers. The Doctor misunderstood George's letter, and sent it on to Stephen. Two days after George was told of Stephen's collapse (E. J. Phillips told him by letter), George wrote to Phillips:

> 'After today, thank God, I take a rest. Although I have seen great results I have never been more worn out than this place (Manchester).'

During the Manchester Crusade he had paid a visit to Oldham and had to face the problem of having his nephew, Edward preaching, not only in the same town on the same night but of being almost next door. Four days later he reported; 'Since the close of the Campaign I have not been feeling too well'.

A church was established in Manchester but it did not join the Direct Government section; after a few years the work folded up.

In 1935 George's year began north of the border. There were meetings in Aberdeen from the end of January to late in February.

On February 21st, a group which included the Revival Party as well as E.J. Phillips and Percy Corry left for Egypt and Palestine. They were away for forty-eight days and they had a wonderful time visiting Bible Lands. On their return, George sent E.J. Phillips a cheque as, 'a small token of our regard for the untiring services you have rendered to us in private and otherwise'.

George continued with his evangelistic work in England when he returned. In June he was in Stockton for a few days with meetings in the Constitution Hall. There were also meetings in Middlesborough and Darlington. Both places joined the Local Government group, but they were both small churches. At the end of July he began at Scunthorpe; he returned there again in August.

On August 6th he opened in Lincoln in a tent. It was to be the most successful of his British Campaigns that year; it was still modest compared with previous years. On the first night a stately looking gentleman, who was seated with a small group of ladies, was gripped by George's preaching. When George made the appeal, the gentleman raised his hand in response to the Gospel invitation. Unknown to the Revival Party at the time, and subsequently kept private, it was discovered that the gentleman was Lord Belhavon and Stenton, C.I.E. It was not the first time that a member of the aristocracy had been attracted to George's ministry, but it was probably his most aristocratic convert.

A few years earlier, Lady Brownlow Cecil had helped to give out invitations to his meetings in Exeter. In Eastbourne the emphasis on Divine Healing drew a curious crowd to the Winter Garden. On that occasion they included Sir Arthur Conan Doyle, creator of Sherlock Holmes. In Eastbourne also Lady Holman, wife of Lieut. General Sir H.C. Holman, was healed of an eye complaint. Her daughter,Joan married James McWhirter of the Revival Party.

The number of converts in Lincoln rose to just over 300 and a church was established. This church also joined the Local Government group. The work was never large; when they officially joined in January 1936 there were forty-six members.

At this time George started the World Revival Crusade. This organisation took over the financial responsibility for his Crusades. According to his own statement, the experience in Switzerland in 1934, and more especially in Bible Lands in 1935 gave him the idea of seeking to establish a wider fellowship that could have a world-wide membership.

He returned from Switzerland in October after being there for about five weeks. In that time huge crowds met him in every place, many failing to get in to the halls that were used. The number of converts was double that of 1934. At Berne there were 164 in the first meeting. At Bienne the State Church was crowded and there were fifty-three converts. It was the same in every place they visited, in France and Switzerland. The tally of converts reached 12,000. This time the party consisted of a dozen ministers. George's secretary and pianist, Albert Edsor wrote:

> 'The two largest churches in La Chaux-Fonds packed to suffocation and over one thousand souls saved. Surely this must be the greatest revival ever witnessed in this lovely land.'

On his return to Britain, George went to Bristol where he

held meetings for Percy Parker, a former Congregational minister who had joined Elim a few years before. Parker's Bible Correspondence Course was used by the Elim Bible College. Parker had become dissatisfied with some aspects of the Elim work and had left for a time but then rejoined. The response in Bristol was disappointing. Most of those who came to the meetings were believers. The Empire Theatre was booked for three Sunday evenings and at the first of these meetings there were sixty-four converts. On the following Sunday they recorded another thirty-five but, in contrast to the huge success in Switzerland, the numbers were very small and the response disappointing.

Other events at the same time also caused some concern. One of the first batch of students who had been in the first class at the Bible College at the end of 1925, Jesse Lees, left at the end of October and joined the Church of England. Another of their very able ministers (who had been with the party in Switzerland in 1935), William G Channon, and his wife Wilhemina (also a very able preacher) left and joined the Baptists, first in Ireland; he subsequently became a leading Baptist minister and pastor of Spurgeon's Tabernacle, London. His early association with George Jeffreys and the Elim work was hardly acknowledged in later years.

The financial returns from the Manchester Crusade were completed at this time and they revealed a loss of several hundred pounds (Very few of George's Crusades lost money. They usually left a small balance).

The Lincoln Church was giving cause for concern also. In December, George complained:

> 'As usual they expect me to build them a church and to subsidise them as I have done for years in other places, but I am doing nothing of the kind not even if they go to smithereens.'

The year ended with a brief visit to Bath, where over the weekend of December 7th-8th they recorded thirty-six converts. There were one night stands in Swindon and

Salisbury and at Salisbury several members of the local council came to the meeting.

At the beginning of 1936 George was then in Glasgow, two days in Aberdeen at the beginning of February were followed by four days in Dundee where there were forty-two converts. One night stands in Dunfermline and Kilsyth were hardly enough to move either place. A return to Edinburgh and Greenock, even though they drew good numbers did not produce the same response as his first visit.

In March, he made another of his frequent visits to Blackpool. There were 470 converts there. In the final meeting in the Opera House on April 5th there were seventy-seven converts. Yet, once again, in Blackpool he had to suffer the embarrassment of having his nephew, Eddie, who was living in St. Anne's, holding meetings at the same time. On this occasion Eddie went so far as to advertise that he would speak on 'The right use of the tongue'. Poor George, he did not know how he was going to face the press.

This year was Elim's 'Coming of Age'. A special effort was made to reduce the debts on Elim buildings and a Debt Clearance Fund was launched late in 1935. The small income of the first year rose to £6,870 in Jubilee Year (1936). In the following year it dropped to just over £2,000 but in 1938 there was a record figure of £13,794 (including a single donation of £6,200). The lady who gave this gift was moved to do so by an article in the *Evangel* by Ralph M. Riggs, later to be the General Superintendent of the American Assemblies of God. The article on tithing contained the following statements:

> 'If our present possessions have been purchased with untithed money then one tenth of all we own has been bought with God's money and we should pay that back unto Him. Figure it up carefully. Buy God's interest out of your capital stock and pay that sum directly into His Kingdom work.'

This article appeared on March 25th, 1938. In the May 6th issue, George was able to report that they had received the gift in answer to prayer.

On his birthday in 1936 George was presented with an illuminated address. It was signed by the staff and principal officers at Elim Headquarters. George was forty-seven years of age. Elim was celebrating its twenty-first year. During the meetings in the Royal Albert Hall on Whit Monday, George was presented with another illuminated address. It was signed by eleven laymen who represented the 209 churches in Britain. The ministers had contributed a gift of £72 which was given to George as a token of their appreciation for his ministry.

George had agreed to undertake a Jubilee tour of the churches which was to take up most of May. He was to stay in most places for one night only and some places were only given a few days notice of his visit. He ranged over a wide area from Liverpool to Nottingham. The best response was in Southport where they had a congregation of 900, with forty-seven converts on April 29th. In Manchester, on May 20th, he reported:

> 'Feeling the anointing of the Spirit so much, I spoke for over an hour, and no less than forty-four souls decided for Christ.'

In June, he was in Wales. First at Neath, where twenty-seven year old P.S. Brewster, one of his East Ham converts, a man who eventually became Secretary to the World Pentecostal Conference and Elim's Secretary-General, was responsible for establishing a church following a campaign. Brewster became a very successful evangelist and over a period of years founded some forty churches. There were also meetings in Llanelly when they used the Ritz Palis de Danse. Brief visits were made to Cardiff and Swansea.

On July 1st, George officiated at the wedding of James McWhirter in Eastbourne. Later that month he made another of his regular visits to Keswick where he attended the Convention.

On August 9th he was in Belfast and drew great crowds to meetings in the tent at Annandale Embankment. For the three final days they hired the recently opened King's Hall, Balmoral, the largest public hall in Ireland. It had been used for exhibitions and boxing matches. The council laid on extra trams and buses and even reduced the bus fares for the occasion. There were such crowds; it was estimated that 10,000 were in the final meeting. There were 750 converts during three weeks. In the last meeting George's pulpit was a boxing ring that was to be used for a fight on the following day.

On September 5th they hired the Crystal Palace for their Coming of Age Celebrations. Many of the workers from the early days were present. A programme was presented that told the story of the growth and development of the work. It was the last time that they would be able to use the building as it was destroyed two months later. Elim had come of age as far as the number of years it had existed but the next few years were to be years of difficulty.

16: Clouds of Conflict

In 1936, after a visit to Guernsey, George travelled to Switzerland. In Baden and in Lausanne crowds numbering several thousand came to hear them. During a period of two weeks 2,000 converts were recorded. In one meeting there were said to be thirty-two nationalities present.

On November 12th, the Principal officiated at the marriage of E. J. Phillips in Clapham. The members of the Revival Party gave E. J. and Molly a desk and a bookcase: the desk bears the inscription:

> 'To our true friend Pastor E. J. Phillips from Principal George Jeffreys and the Revival Party on the occasion of his marriage November 12th 1936.'

Relations between the two men could not have been better. Both men had given themselves unsparingly to the task of building up the Elim work. George as an evangelist who travelled far and wide establishing many churches; E. J. however, spent most of his time behind his office desk where he served as Secretary-General dealing with a huge volume of correspondence on all aspects of the work, both legal and financial. He was often in the office at 7 a.m. and at times the lights were still burning after 10 p.m. He kept in very close touch with the Principal and they hardly ever made decisions of any importance without consulting each other. The suggestion has been made that George did not know what was going on within the Movement that he had founded. That is without any foundation. Even a brief acquaintance with the correspondence will show that this is untrue.

A short time after E. J. Phillips was married he received a letter from the Principal. The letter indicated that it had been composed before George had been told of E. J.'s intention to marry. When he learned of this he delayed sending the letter. Now that E. J. and his new wife were settled in their new home, George felt that he could write to him.

The letter was dated December 9th, 1936. The Principal offered to relinquish his position. He went on to outline the reasons for this dramatic decision:

> 'I shall be released from what I feel is a burden.
> Be more free to follow my spiritual calling.
> . . . allow some of our splendid ministers to be elected to the Executive . . .'

He went on to state that he had no intention of being severed from Elim, but that he simply wanted to be released from responsibilities of leadership and from the business side of the work.

E. J. Phillips went to see him on the same day and he kept notes of their conversation. George told him that he was worried about three things in particular. First the debts; secondly by the local trustees, and also for the ministers who would be hurt if there was a split in the Conference. He made it clear that he did not wish this to go outside the Executive Council. He further stated that this was not meant to be an ultimatum. He might be prepared to stay on as leader if certain conditions could be met; he told E. J. that he would write to him but that he must treat the letter as confidential. George said that he preferred to resign but he was prepared to remain as a 'spiritual father'.

On December 15th, 1936, George wrote a two page letter. He attached a further four pages containing his proposals. In these he stated once more that he wished to be relieved of the responsibility of leadership and to be free from the business side of work without any qualifications whatsoever. He was prepared to allow the new Executive to shape its own policy without any interference or dictation from him. He further declared:

> 'I have no thought of leaving the work, on the contrary, I have every intention of going ahead with you all, in spreading the glorious work of deepening the confidence we have in each other.'

As for his confidence in the Executive, he wrote:

> 'Let me say from the depth of my heart that no leader could be surrounded by a more devoted, self-sacrificing, and trustworthy band of men than those who surround me. It is this knowledge that prompts me to hand over the work without the thought of settling the terms for the withdrawal of myself.'

George's new proposals involved dividing the Direct Government section of the work into two sections. The one would be a 'Jubilee Concentration', whose churches would all be self-supporting. The other would be a 'Forward Movement' that would bring together all other churches at present in the Direct Government group (those which were not self-supporting). Any who wished to join from any other group would be put in the Forward Movement. It would also include all future churches as these were established. This seemed to have been a temporary solution, as George stated that when all debts were paid, both sections could revert to the present way of working.

E. J. Phillips waited for two weeks before replying in detail to the proposals. He had, however, spoken to the Principal by phone, pointing out some of the difficulties of the scheme. The objections were that it would involve extensive alterations to the Deed Poll, which would be an expensive and long-drawn-out business. It would divide the work and the two sections might easily drift apart. It would be impossible to govern without a central authority. All the best men would be in one group and all inexperienced and unsuccessful in the other, yet George was proposing to put the future of Elim in the latter group. With regard to the Principal's proposed resignation, Phillips and the other elected members of the Council were very concerned. E. J. told George:

> 'There is not the slightest doubt that it would be a real blow to the work. Whatever explanation you might make, people will always believe that there is something behind it . . . I trust therefore that you will give us the welcome assurance that you will remain as leader of the work.'

Another dimension was added when George proposed to issue a magazine to enable him to keep in touch with members of his recently formed World Revival Crusade. E. J. talked over these proposals with him and it became clear that the proposed new magazine would give space to George's views on British Israelism. During the interview, George told Phillips that James McWhirter was going to bring out a book on Palestine at Easter. This was to be issued by an outside publisher (Methuen) and when it did appear it caused a good deal of bad feeling. That was just one more factor in an increasingly complicated matter that would drag on for some time.

Letters continued from both sides. It soon became clear that although these letters were at first private correspondence between two men; they soon became official letters between the Principal and the elected members of the Council. An unofficial meeting of all the elected members of the Council, together with F. B. Phillips, manager of the Publishing Company (brother of E. J.) and Douglas B. Gray, leader of the London Crusade Choir, met to discuss the possible publication of George's new paper. They were all very concerned about this and the implications of the other aspects of his proposed action. They reminded him that he had told the Young People's Conference, 'Forsake not the work of thine hands' (Psalm 138:8). E. J. Phillips went on to say:

> 'The Elim Movement today is just what you made it. You have therefore a moral responsibility to stand by it. You have been the means, under God in bringing the Elim child into the world and you are therefore committing a grave wrong on threatening to desert it. We all therefore want to plead with you prayerfully to consider the whole matter again before you take any irreversible step.'

Also included in their list of objections, was the fact, in their view, that another organisation (The World Revival Crusade with its own paper and the possibility of its own 'Fellowship Centres') would draw away finance from Elim. They added that such an organisation would, 'propagate doctrines which were considered unscriptural by the majority of Elim people.'

George wrote back by return and seized upon the last point, demanding to know the meaning of this phrase. E. J. replied that in using these words he had meant the teaching of B.I. which had been rejected by the Ministerial Conference.

Two days later George wrote again:

> 'I am more convinced than ever, that the message I told you of, 'Set your house in order', is a divine command, which I personally dare not disobey.'

The Principal still maintained that he had no intention of leaving Elim. From that time, if not before, the dye was cast. It would take a year or two before the final break came; there would be attempts at reconciliation, with attempted mediation from a number of friends at different times, but it was all to no avail. George Jeffreys, the Founder and leader of Elim eventually left the work that he had started. It is a complicated and tragic story. It gives us no joy to record this fact, but something must be said on the matter.

17: A House Divided

The story of the division in Elim, often referred to as 'the split' has been the subject of several publications. These include the contribution of sociologist, Bryan Wilson. His book, *Sects and Society,* Heinemann,1961, is taken from a Ph.D. thesis that dealt with three religious groups, of which Elim formed the most important (and the most often quoted section). Wilson's main interest was in sociology and that of the sociology of religious sects in particular. He is now a recognised authority on the subject. That does not prevent us from saying that, as far as his analysis of the cause of the split are concerned, his conclusions are very wide of the mark. We do not blame Wilson for this. There are errors of fact (sometimes as many as three to a single page) that have not been corrected in the American reprint. Wilson's problem was that he did not have access to most of the relevant material: letters, minutes etc., dealing with this period. The only material that he used, apart from Noel Brooks', *Fight for the Faith and Freedom,* Pattern, 1948, was a single pamphlet written by George Jeffreys, *Why I Resigned from the Elim Movement.* Yet he must have known that there was a mass of printed material on the other side. In fact the total amount of printed material in the form of pamphlets extends to more than 100 pages in some thirty-four separate leaflets, some as long as eight pages in length. In fact Wilson committed one of the elementary errors that one would expect from an inexperienced student. He simply turned up on the doorstep of the Elim Headquarters in Clarence Avenue at some time in 1953. He made no appointment and only spoke to a very junior member of staff, who knew very little about the issues that were involved. It is outside the present writer's object or intention to give a detailed account of all aspects of the controversy. There is enough material to fill a large volume; in addition to the pamphlets there are printed letters; articles in *The Pattern* as well as Minutes of Conference.

Another account of the controversy is given by Noel Brooks. Brooks founded the Parkgate Church, Rotherham and joined Elim under one of the Local Government groups in 1934. He resigned in January 1938 because he, 'no longer accepts the Pentecostal position'. He joined the Baptists for a time and subsequently, for a short time, he was pastor of Elim Evangelical Church, Pembroke Hall, Tennell St., Bristol.

Wilson acknowledged that Noel Brooks' account presented a 'partisan defence' of the position. In fact it is worth recording that the author tried to have the book withdrawn from sale and he later regretted that it had ever been written. He subsequently became a minister of the Pentecostal Holiness Church and took an external B.D. at London University. He was one of a number of men who were in the Bible Pattern Church Fellowship that was formed by George Jeffreys in Nottingham in November 1940.

It is not my purpose to prove that George Jeffreys was wrong (though after reading through all the material I am convinced that the action he took was mistaken). Neither am I suggesting that everything Elim did was correct. They could be stubborn and unbelievably pedantic. My chief concern is to show what effect these events had upon the evangelistic and church-planting work of George Jeffreys. There can be no doubt that they drained his energy and diverted his attention away from his God-appointed task of winning multitudes to Christ.

The basic problem was not his views on prophetic interpretation, but his constant change of mind. The files of the Elim archives are full of one scheme after another that George Jeffreys advanced in a vain attempt to find what he called, the biblical pattern of church government. Anyone with even a smattering of knowledge of church history will be aware that this was not the first time the precise form of government to be employed in the church was to be a divisive issue. It was an issue at the time of the Reformation. It may not have been the main issue, but men were sent to the stake for holding views that were contrary to the generally accepted standard of the time. In the Commonwealth period, good men found themselves ranged on both sides of the issue. There was an equal sincerity on both sides. It was perhaps unfortunate that George Jeffreys had a very limited understanding of Church History, he was essentially a pragmatist.

The growing pressure and the Principal's threatened resignation had a very serious effect upon E. J. Phillips. He was already grossly overworked. A few years before he had sought to find a suitable assistant to take over the responsibility for the property side of the work. He had wanted to employ Don House of Bournemouth but George Jeffreys was not in agreement. Don House subsequently became President of the Auctioneers Association of Great Britain. He served on a number of Elim committees in later years and became a leading layman. A number of young men helped in the office, but they only held junior positions. A lot of extra work was created by the many schemes and plans that George suggested for the government of the work. Most of these came to nothing.

E. J. Phillips was taken ill and he had to leave office. He was present at the executive meetings in March and in May 1937 (the Principal was absent). A special meeting was convened at Phillips's home on July 29th and he agreed to pass over a lot of his work to other members of the Council, particularly to Hathaway and Boulton. On Friday, July 30th, a specialist called to see Mr Phillips and he strongly advised that he should be moved into hospital. He was taken to the Royal Northern Hospital in Holloway Road at mid-day. The hospital phoned his wife on the following day to report that his condition was causing some anxiety. Following an X ray and an examination it became known that his left lung was affected. He would have to spend six to nine months in a Sanatorium. He did not attend any meetings of the Executive Council between May 1937 and May 1938.

During these meetings it became clear that the financial returns from the churches in 1937 were expected to show a deficit of £750 to £1,000 in spite of a legacy of £1,000. The Executive meeting, which began on October 11th, went on for ten days. They proposed drastic action to try to remedy the situation. As the Constitution required them to inform the Secretary-General, W.G. Hathaway wrote to E. J. Phillips in the Royal National Hospital, Ventnor. They told him that they were proposing to put all ministers, except those in the top forty churches, on 'faith lines'. It meant that they would be without any salary from Headquarters. As it turned out there were only thirty-three churches who were able to support a minister out of their own income, though several of the larger churches could have supported several. At that time all ministers (except the Principal and some of his Revival Party) were paid from Headquarters. One of the few good things to come out of the confusion of that time was that Church Treasurers were permitted to pay their local expenses, including their minister's salary.

To have put thirty-three ministers on a regular salary and to have left the remaining eighty-seven without any certain income at all was indeed a drastic measure, The proposal entailed the larger number leaving the direct Government section all together. The thirty or so of the more senior ministers would control the Conference. The Principal wanted to sell the Bible College. There were very few students there at that time as they had not been encouraged to apply owing to the lack of openings with the reduction of George's pioneering work. The College however continued to make a profit after paying their mortgage. To have sold the premises at such a time would have been disastrous.

In George's view there was a serious financial crisis in the Movement. When he went to work in the office after E. J.

Phillips was taken ill he calculated that Elim's total debts amounted to £44,000. On this basis he calculated that if they were to try and pay this all off at the current rate (the Building Societies were charging interest of £12 per month for a deficit of a thousand pounds) it would take fifteen years to clear. The actual figure was £41,808 at October 31st, 1937 (the end of the financial year). There had been a reduction of almost £4,000 since the previous year. In fact the total debts had been reduced every year since 1934 and there was no reason to think that this would not continue. These debts were incurred in buying up churches and houses as the movement had rapidly expanded. It needs to be said, loud and clear: THERE WAS NO FINANCIAL CRISIS IN ELIM IN 1937. The audited accounts (which were published) make this very clear. None of these debts had been called in and the assets at that time were valued at some £200,000 at least.

Writing to George Jeffreys at the end of June 1938, E. J. Phillips said:

> 'I maintain that there was no financial crisis. Those who feared a financial crisis had practically no knowledge of book-keeping.'

The sickness of E. J. Phillips and his prolonged absence from the office was a serious matter. His office was left virtually undisturbed during that time.

In December 1937 George Jeffreys collapsed with a breakdown. In January 1938 they had to call for a special time of prayer for the Principal. On the first day of the year, W. G. Hathaway wrote to all the ministers:

> 'The Principal's physical condition is giving us cause for grave concern. The strain of the past twelve months has taken its toll of his strength, and his health is in danger of giving way as a result.
>
> We feel it is most urgent that you should call your people to definite believing prayer on behalf of our beloved leader, that the living touch of God may rest upon him in

his hour of need. God has wonderfully used him in the past to minister to thousands in need throughout the world. It is for us now to stand with him and minister to him by our believing prayers.

The monthly day of prayer will be held on Tuesday next, 4th inst., and we would like special prayer in your church for our beloved leader.

Praying God will bless and guide us all at this time.'

There had been a marked deterioration in the Principal's condition and so his friends and close associates, Albert Edsor and Robert E. Darragh were called to his hospital bedside at 6 a.m. after being roused by a policeman. At the end of January 1938 the *Elim Evangel* was able to report:

'We are happy to report that as a result of earnest and united prayer on his behalf there is a definite improvement in the condition of our beloved leader. For twenty-three years Principal George Jeffreys has stood at the forefront of the battle, bearing the strain of leadership in this progressive spiritual movement, of which he has been the pioneer . . . Principal has been the target of bitter attack . . . In addition to this there has been the burden of making suitable provision for the ever-increasing number of converts who have been won to Christ as a result of his ministry. This has meant shouldering heavy financial responsibilities, the constant accumulation of which has taken its toll on his strength, and contributed to his present condition.'

As things turned out, his health was never to be as robust again. He suffered from diabetes for the rest of his life. He would hold a good number of Crusades in the years that followed, both at home and on the continent, but as far as Elim was concerned he was nearing the end of the period of his real and notable success as an evangelist and church planter.

Yet, writing about the experience some years later, George saw his illness as almost providential:

'The sudden illness of the Secretary-General followed closely by mine, and I believe that under the circumstances it had to be, in order to bring about the opportunity for an exacting examination of ourselves and the rapidly growing organisation.'

He went on to state:

'In my illness I had an experience which revealed the things I would suffer in the oncoming struggle to free the churches from the legal system that had bound them . . . What I saw made me determined, regardless of cost, to reform it or to renounce it.'

That is how he explained it eight years later. At the time, writing under his own name in the *Elim Evangel* on April 29th, 1938 he told a different story.

'Some day I shall be able to write the whole story of my breakdown and God's remarkable deliverance in answer to your prayers.
The threatened financial crisis with its apparently inevitable upheaval which brought about my physical breakdown.'

He went on to outline the actions that the Executive Council were taking to try and wipe out all the debts. In the following issue they were able to report the largest single gift to the Alliance to date.

It seemed now that the Revivalist had set his mind also on becoming a Reformer. As a revivalist he was without equal; as a reformer he was a disaster. Let James McWhirter, who knew him as well as anyone give his view of the matter:

'For the record I should tell you something that gives me no joy to relate. George Jeffreys resigned from Elim on an issue of church government. As subsequent events have proved, doing so was a tragedy. Had he remained a

Revivalist and not tried to be a Reformer, he might have gone down in history as one of the greatest . . . What he called a vision was only an illusion.'

The reforms did not come over night. There was an Executive Council of eight other men who had to be convinced, or at least the majority of that number. George had the right to nominate three of the members of the Council (he had wanted four). They held their places by right of his appointment and not by any vote. From 1934 the other four places (apart from the Principal and the Secretary-General) were subject to the votes of the Ministerial Session of the Conference. George withdrew his right to nominate the three for a time in March 1937 (he took this back later). The other members of the Council at this time were W.G. Hathaway, E.C.W. Boulton, P.N. Corry, Joseph Smith, Charles Kingston, Robert Mercer and Samuel Gorman.

There was also a larger body that had to be convinced. In the Council George could carry a lot of weight, particularly when his own appointees were on the Council. Persuading the Conference was another matter altogether. Though many of the ministers had been converted as a result of his ministry they were not yes-men, many were prepared to voice their own opinions and convictions. While the fellowship was sweet, the debates were hard. There was plenty of cut and thrust, the ministers who had to pastor the churches after the Principal moved on were not easily swayed.

Prior to the opening of the 1938 Conference, the Principal had circulated a six page duplicated memorandum that contained his suggestions for the future government of work. Basically he put forward two schemes. When the Conference met on September 16th it became clear that there was a difficult few days ahead of the assembled ministers. On the second day, the Journal recorded that:

'The Principal objected . . . and read to the Conference

> an ultimatum, stating that the Conference must introduce a new legislative body with lay representation or else he would have no alternative but to resign in six months time . . . if such a proposal were not introduced, he would go to the churches on this issue and tell them why he resigned.'

The feeling of the Conference were very tense. When they met again in the afternoon, the Journal report continued:

> 'The Principal expressed the strong conviction that there was a strong demand in our churches for Lay Representation. This was challenged by some of those present. On a show of hands being taken, eight indicated a desire in their churches for Lay Representation, four being from Ireland.'

When the matter was put to the vote, sixteen were in favour, fifty-nine were against, with seven abstaining.

On the Thursday, the Principal withdrew his proposed resignation and a number of major changes were accepted. Each of these gave greater power to the Conference.

Once his health had improved sufficiently the Principal resumed his evangelistic activity. On June 4th he began a campaign in a tent in Colwyn Bay. On Whit Monday the tent was seriously damaged in an eighty mile per hour gale and they had to hire various halls while a replacement was being obtained. A total of some 500 converts were recorded during the period but no permanent Elim work was established.

At the end of July he pitched his tent on the Fairground, Commercial Road, Portsmouth. During a period of more than two months he counted some 900 converts. The original church that was established in 1927 was strengthened but not greatly enlarged as a result.

After the Conference George went back to Nottingham for nine days, beginning on October 8th. On this visit he was to record some 800 converts who helped to fill the huge City Temple, Halifax Place.

Apart from these efforts, two in established churches and one in a new area that left no new church, this was almost the total extent of George's labours during the year. His illness would explain some of the lessening of his activity but there were other, more deep seated reasons.

In 1939 the same pattern was followed. In February he returned to Carlisle. There were good meetings there, but he did not manage to captivate the city as he had done a dozen years before. It is perhaps worth noting that all of the places that he returned to at this time were to become the places where he found the greatest measure of support when, a few years later, he started a rival organisation.

In April and May he went to Ilfracombe for meetings but no permanent work was established as a result of these efforts. While he was there the storm clouds of war were building up over Europe. E. J. Phillips wrote to him to say that he was very concerned about the possibility of the outbreak of war. He wanted to make Elim's position clear on their attitude to the question of taking up arms. During the First World War a number of men who were later to become leaders in the Assemblies of God had been imprisoned or had to do some form of directed land work when they registered as objectors. Phillips wrote to say that he proposed to publish the Resolution of the 1935 Conference on the subject in the next available issue of the *Elim Evangel.* The Resolution said:

> 'That while this General Conference of the Elim Foursquare Gospel Alliance affirms its loyalty to His Majesty the King and to the government of this land, it believes that the Church of Jesus Christ which is called from the world to preach the Gospel of salvation and peace to all men is based on spiritual principles which are incompatible with the Christian's participation in war. It considers however, that this is a matter which every

> believer should settle for himself in the light of the word of God.'

When the matter was put to the vote there were 100 in favour and only two against (these were John Leech K.C. and James McWhirter). There was one abstention – George Jeffreys.

Now, in April 1939, E. J. Phillips was simply proposing that this Resolution (that had previously been printed in the *Elim Evangel* in November 1935) should be issued once again to help those who might be called up in the near future.

George wired from Ilfracombe:

> 'Too important to decide without Executive meeting to discuss.'

When Phillips received the telegram he wrote to explain that he was only going to print the Resolution but George sent another telegram and a letter to press home his point:

> 'Letter received as all Executive members are involved each one should be consulted on this important step.'

His letter confirms this (though the wording is different):

> 'Cannot take personal responsibility. Ministers should be consulted. They have to face their churches and any resultant repercussions. Prince.'

He said that publishing the 1935 Resolution would do harm:

> 'It would split out churches from one end to the other, for there are opposite viewpoints on the question throughout the land.'

The Resolution was printed on May 12th. This made clear

the view of the Conference in 1935. Whether that was still the view in 1939 was another matter. In the years between those two dates the international climate had changed considerably. It was in 1935 that the debate had taken place at the Oxford Union when a majority had expressed the view that taking up arms to fight was wrong. The Elim Conference of 1935 was somewhat unusual in that they also voted against mixed bathing!

After war was declared a few of the younger ministers left to join the services. One of them was with Winston Churchill's party at the Yalta Conference. Another, with the Christian names of Horatio Kitchener also signed on. Dr Frank Weston, a Crusade Commissioner went down when his ship, on which he was serving as a Surgeon Commander was sunk in the first few months of the war.

On the other side, Frederick B. Phillips, brother of E. J. and manager of the Elim Publishing Company had written a book in March 1936, *Is War Christian?*. It was published by the Elim Publishing Company and was well publicised in the Elim papers.

James McWhirter of the Revival Party published a strongly worded pamphlet, *The Bible and War*, Covenant Publishing Company, 1940. McWhirter had been converted in Ireland in 1916 when he was a boy soldier. In 1936 he had married the daughter of a retired Lieutenant-General, who wrote the forward to the booklet.

Once again the Principal found himself in the minority and on opposite sides from his Secretary-General. To allude to Samuel Taylor Coleridge's poem *Christabel*:

> 'Alas they had been friends of youth,
> But whispering tongues can poison truth . . .
> And to be wroth with one we love
> Doth work like madness in the brain.'

The two men had been so close for many years; there had been such an understanding and trust between them. Now they began to differ once more, and again this was on vital issues. To depict this, as some have done, as a clash between a charismatic leader and a bureaucratic official is to over simplify the whole situation. In the late fifties and early sixties sociologists and others were rather inclined to pigeon-hole into neat little catagories, but the pattern of human behaviour is much more complex. George Jeffreys had been the easiest of men to work with in the early period. Now, largely as a result of his illness, and possibly also through the influence of others there was a distinct change in his attitude. The letters make this very clear; what had begun as formal letters between two friends with the same interests, now became carefully written for public consumption. They were no longer letters, they were tracts, and they grew in length and increased in frequency. In such a course there could only be one conclusion; it would end in a final break.

George Jeffreys was now almost alone on the Council (Robert Mercer supported him for most of the short time he was the Principal's nominee). In the General Conference he had little support; in the Ministerial Conference even less. It was not an easy situation. Some men had been so blessed through his ministry they believed that he could do no wrong; some were prepared to follow him almost anywhere.

The 1938 Conference had been difficult; the Conference of 1939 would be even more difficult. George had spent July and August in a tent Crusade in Worthing. The Conference was due to open in September. When the notices had been sent out giving the date as Monday, September 18th, the Principal indicated that he would not attend. E.J. Phillips wrote to him to impress upon him the importance of his attendance. In the meantime there was a marked deterioration in the situation in Europe and the opening date of the Conference was postponed.

War was declared on Sunday, September 3rd. On that morning W.E. Sangster began his ministry at Westminster Central Hall, London. The morning service at the Elim Church, Park Crescent, Clapham was interrupted by the air raid siren as Percy Corry was reading Romans chapter eight. Later in the war the church was destroyed after being damaged on an earlier occasion.

The delayed Conference began on November 20th and it continued for two weeks until December 1st. Prior to the opening of the Conference the Executive Council had given permission for the Principal to circulate his ideas for a change in the government of the movement. He had duplicated a seven page paper that was sent out to 100 ministers. He also enclosed a list of questions and asked them to indicate what changes they wanted. He asked them to write to him to tell him what they wanted. The Council did not see these papers before they were sent out. On the same day (July 11th) the Council sent out their proposals that were to form the basis for discussion at the Conference.

By the end of July, half of the ministers had replied to the Principal's circular and he followed it up with a further short paper. It really was not the right way to conduct business or to make changes. The seven members of the Council (Phillips, Hathaway, Joseph Smith, Corry, Charles Kingston and Samuel Gorman) wrote to the ministers to express their regret at the contents of the Principal's letter. They complained that it contained inaccurate statements that demanded a reply, point by point. In their letter of August 3rd, they said:

> 'However, after prayerful consideration of the situation, we are convinced that it would not be in the best interests of the work to answer by a circular letter which would undoubtedly lead to a prolonged correspondence between the Principal and ourselves continuing right up to the Conference. Such correspondence would accentuate the tension already existing and would perhaps lead to bitter controversy . . .
> Rather than allow this to take place, we have decided to answer the Principal's letter by a full statement to the Ministerial Conference in September . . .'

They went on to say that they, 'deeply deplored the continual agitation which has persisted for several years, and which has brought this work which God has so much blessed, almost to a state of chaos'. They said that they would 'be guided by the wishes of the Ministers in a proper Constitutional manner, and not in an unconstitutional way in which matters were being forced upon them'.

George's reaction to this letter was swift, he immediately wrote to all the ministers in another circular telling them that if he had met the Executive at that time, the breach might have been avoided. The Council did not send their reply until August 15th (several of them had been on holiday at the time). Some of them sent letters to the Principal. They were still reluctant to drag the discussion into a publication or to make it a public discussion. They even went so far as to outline some of the dangers that such a course of action might have. The only result of their action was yet more circulars. He went so far as to publish selected Minutes of the meetings of the Executive Council of May 22nd (It was the last meeting of the Council that he ever attended). At that meeting the Council had agreed that he should send out a list of his proposals to the ministers. He also agreed that he would show them a Draft of these proposals before sending them out but he did not do this.

When the Council met the next time the Principal did not attend. He also said that he was in 'soul-saving work in Worthing, and secondly, I did not want to run the risk of holding up the Executive by a possible discussion of what or was not a major issue'.

He sent out another six circulars before the end of the year; they amounted to seventeen pages in length. When the Conference was eventually convened he was not present for most of the sessions. Some of the time he sat in the minister's vestry in the Clapham Church or stayed in his home, half a mile away. The Conference appointed a delegation to wait on him. First a group of three or four, then later this was increased to ten men of his chosing. They carried messages to and fro for several days. It was not the best way to bring about any sort of agreement and it was a very strange way to conduct business.

On Tuesday morning of the first week, E. J. Phillips began to put the Executive's answer to the Principal's circular letter of July 11th. The minutes state:

> 'There was continual discussion of the situation in Elim owing to the divergent views on policy between the majority of the Executive Council and the majority of the Ministerial Conference on the one hand and the Principal and the minority on the other hand. Mr Phillips showed the adverse effect on the Movement that the various changes which had been introduced, and also through the cessation of definite pioneer evangelism. It was felt by the majority present that thc Principal should bc present as it was impossible to continue discussions . . . without him being present. They reported that he declined to come to the Conference at that time.'

On the Wednesday afternoon of the second week, the Principal replied to the points made by the Conference. He expressed the view that he could not be curtailed in his own personal liberty; he would not agree to curtail his efforts at influencing the issues by means of circular, printed matter or personal canvassing outside the Conference. He did declare however:

> 'It is not my intention however, to disturb the Constitution of the Elim Alliance if amended in accordance with the suggested changes, nor to disturb the peace of its churches.'

At this point, the Conference refused to go any further by this unsatisfactory and indirect method of negotiation by delegation. They insisted that he should be present. In the evening he came and sat in the minister's vestry, while the Conference met in the Minor Hall of the Clapham Church.

The Conference gave way on a number of items, but by now the Principal was relying more and more on the wishes of his lay advisers. In fact he did not seem to know what he did want. He also said that he, 'had no idea what his laymen wanted'. It was clear that further negotiation on this subject was impossible. The Principal was therefore asked to give his final views to the Conference. They gave him twenty-eight days to give his decision. This was later reduced to seven days. They asked for three things:

1. That he limit the number of laymen with whom he consulted to six (it was believed that this was the current number of his lay consultants).
2. That he undertake not to contend against the Constitution by means of circular letter, printed matter or organised effort.
3. They asked him to sign an agreement embodying the terms of the agreement at the Conference.

When the matter was put to the vote, out of the ninety-four who were present, seventy-nine were in favour, seven against: there were eight abstentions.

On the Friday morning the Principal came in and read a staement announcing his resignation from the Alliance and from the Elim Church proper. After handing over his resignation he left the meeting. The Conference then discussed his resignation. After expressing their appreciation for his many years of service, they earnestly desired him to accept the office of Moderator or spiritual leader of the Alliance, to remain also as Principal of the Bible College. This was passed with seventy in favour, ten against and ten abstentions (most of the latter being members of the delegation).

The resignation of the Principal altered the whole position of the Conference, who then went on to discuss all of his proposed alterations. They agreed to six of his eight points and conceded something on one of the others. The matter of Lay Representation was left for the time being.

When the ministers returned to their churches at the end of the Conference they did not report the Principal's resignation right away. On December 5th they were advised by Headquarters in a circular letter. It said:

'Principal George Jeffreys, who for some time has

intimated his desire along these lines, has resigned from the Executive Council, and is thus released from the business side of the work. This will free him more fully for his spiritual ministry in the work of the Lord, which God has so signally blessed in the past.'

A few days later, the Principal brought out a pamphlet, *Why I resigned from the Elim Movement.* On December 20th, the Executive Council published, *A Reply.* These were the first salvos in a pamphlet war that went on, at least in George's case, for the next seven years.

It has to be admitted that the Elim report was not strictly honest. The Principal had resigned as a minister, and, consequently he was no longer a member of the Council. They were in a difficult position. Although he had resigned, he had promised to reconsider the position of Moderator, so there was a slight possibility that he might return. It may have been better if they had come out with the truth from the start. As things turned out these things were brought to the attention of many of the churches all too soon. First by the widespread distribution of the pamphlet, *Why I Resigned,* and the active campaign by the Principal. He went around the churches in an endeavour to meet the people and to put his case. The Elim Church buildings were closed to him and so he hired public halls and announced the fact in the local papers.

In Carlisle they put a misleading notice in the local paper. It was placed right next to John Woodhead's notice for his Sunday night meeting.

In York, they engaged a hall belonging to a college and there were distressing scenes when the local Elim pastor (a very mild natured man) turned up and disputed the Principal's claims. He was in a difficult position for fifty percent of his deacons and many of the trustees sided with the Principal. After the meeting, or more particularly after the report of the meeting had appeared in *The Pattern* (George's own paper) almost all of these men took the Elim side and the York church stood firm.

There were similar stories that could be told of other places. Sometimes it went one way, sometimes the other, but most of the churches remained with Elim. The chief places where George found his support were those towns where he had held a second campaign not long before these events: they were Carlisle, Nottingham, Portsmouth and Worthing. The other churches that supported him were those that were held by him and his friends in trusts and so they had special interest; Brighton, Blackpool, Glasgow and Kensington.

The total number of Alliance ministers who left with the Principal was less than ten. For some of the ministers who left, it meant that they lost their status as ministers of a recognised denomination and this made them liable for military service. As a result, Albert Edsor and Albion Gaunt received call up papers. It put them in a very difficult position. At the time Percy Parker was meeting R.A. Butler (who was the governement minister responsible), to try and get the new group registered as a separate denomination. This helped to precipitate matters. At a meeting in Nottingham on November 28th and 29th, 1940, the new group was formed. At the suggestion of John Leech, they adopted the name of the Bible Pattern Church Fellowship. This was the group through which George Jeffreys was to direct his energies for the remaining years of his life. It was never a very large group and its chief source of income was through the World Revival Crusade, of which George was leader and Director.

The total number of Elim Churches, or groups from Elim Churches who joined the Bible Pattern was not more than twenty. In the years that followed there were some attempts made to bring about a reconciliation but this was not possible during the lifetime of the Principal. He spent some time with E. J. Phillips, only a short time before he died. On the other hand, the last letter that the Principal wrote, or signed before he died was addressed to a minister who had been in the Bible Pattern Fellowship but who had, together with his church, returned to Elim. The relations between the two groups are on a much better footing today and their leading ministers meet with the Elim Executive Council from time to time. A number of their Churches have joined the Elim Church Incorporated in recent years. It is to be hoped that one day there might be a full reconciliation. Many of the things that George Jeffreys wanted are now a regular feature in Elim Churches. There is a greater freedom in the churches today than there was in the past. It saddens me to have to record the details of the last years of George Jeffreys life: things might have been different.

George Jeffreys career leaves one filled with amazement at times. It was a life of contrasts: from a poor home in a back street, to holding huge crowds spellbound. His greatest triumph was in 1939, when he received international recognition when he was invited by Lewi Pethrus to be the chief speaker at the great European Pentecostal Conference in Stockholm, Sweden. The meetings took place from June 5th-12th. There were delegates from many countries; seventy-five from Britain, 160 from Finland, fifty from Denmark and about twenty from Germany (they were arrested on their return). The evening meetings were held in a huge tent and on one night it was said that there were more than 15,000 people present. Amongst those who attended the meetings were Prince Bernadotte, brother of the King and his wife. They were accompanied by the former Swedish Ambassador to the U.S.A.. The ministry of George Jeffreys made a great impression on the gathering.

The visit to Sweden had a profound effect on George Jeffreys. In the Filadelphia Church in Stockholm there was a membership of 5,800 at that time. The Church had been founded by Lewi Pethrus, a former Baptist minister, in 1911 and it was congregational in its government. During his talks with Lewi Pethrus in April 1939 (when Pethrus was in Britain) and during his stay at the Conference in Sweden, George was persuaded that he ought to adopt the Swedish pattern of church government in Britain. Even supposing that there is a single biblical pattern of church government in the New Testament (which we doubt), to seek to impose the system that had been adopted by Lewi Pethrus in Sweden was carrying pragmatism too far. On such an argument, a case could have been made out for the Swedish Pentecostal Church to employ full-time evangelists and open a Bible School for training their ministers. Sweden was not Britain, but, more importantly, George Jeffreys was not another Lewi Pethrus. There were many other factors that had to be considered, not only biblical but sociological and even psychological. As matters turned out, trying to thrust the Swedish pattern on the Elim work had disastrous consequences. Lewi Pethrus was an administrator and pastor (and a good many other things as well); George Jeffreys was an evangelist (and there was none better). Their roles could not be reversed.

We pass over the remaining years of George Jeffreys life in a few words. After he left Elim he spent a time in the wilderness. As far as Britain was concerned he established a few small churches during the fifties. In 1955 he drew large crowds in Wellington Hall, Belfast. His last tent Crusade was in Birmingham in 1955 and although they did purchase a large church afterwards, the work did not last for very long. George's greatest success in the post-war years was on the continent, in France and Switzerland between 1946 and 1950. When the *Picture Post* wrote about him in May 1946, they called him one of the last great revivalists. Yet their report and pictures could only show him ministering to a small group of elderly ladies: things might have been so different. If only the two brothers could have worked together (and their nephews) for a longer period; if only George had stayed on as an evangelist and if he had gone on pioneering new churches even for a few more years, what might have been accomplished?

We regret the way that things turned out in his later years but we must record our tribute to the man (and to his brother) who was the finest and the most successful British evangelist since the time of John Wesley or George Whitfield.

The Movement that he began has survived him. It survived the crisis of his resignation and it is larger and stronger than it was even at the height of his success.

On the Principal's seventieth birthday, in 1959, Robert E Darragh died at his home in Clapham. George survived his friend by almost three years. He died on Friday, January 26th, 1962, a month before his seventy-third birthday. He was mourned by hundreds; he was loved by thousands.